NWO
Documents
Handbook

Bill Kopf

Kopf

ISBN: 9798374563627

Imprint: Independently published

Contents

Kopf

PREFACE

The documents referenced here range from official government white papers to exercises completed by non-governmental organizations. What they share in common is a disdain for national sovereignty and human independence. This will become abundantly clear as the reader proceeds from one document to the next, as will other common themes.

The criteria for whether a document was qualified as admissible into this book are as follows: 1) I'm aware it exists, 2) I have read it, and 3) it is authored by globalists and used to further their agenda toward a universal government. This compilation by no means constitutes the totality of documentation authored by agents of the New World Order, but is rather focused more on those writings that elucidate the subtext of this modern pandemic era and how globalist actors intend to use it to advance their agenda.

Should the reader be at all in doubt of any such thing as a "new world order", I would ask why then would George Bush Jr. and Senior reference it? Or Nelson Rockefeller. Or Henry Kissinger. Or Adolph Hitler. Or Barak Obama. Or Joseph Biden. Why on January 30, 1976 did 32 senators and 92 representatives in Washington D.C. sign The Declaration of *Interdependence* which stated in part, "Our nation is uniquely endowed to play a creative and decisive role in the *new order* which is taking form around us"? They all seem to be convinced that the NWO is in a fact a very real thing. But what is it?

In short, it's an agenda driven by a very powerful cult of rulers that seeks widespread human extermination. Their plan for global depopulation was literally etched in stone as the occult monument known as The Georgia Guidestones, before it was demolished, stated that the world population should be maintained under 500,000,000 which would require the decimation of the entire world as we are currently somewhere around 7.6 billion. This motivation is "in accordance with nature" as the Guidestones state, and you will notice that same Druidic nature worship come out in many of these documents. The spirit of human sacrifice is alive and well and, as usual throughout history, is equated with the health of Mother Earth. Humans must die so that Mother Earth may live.

...because they exchanged the truth about God for a lie and worshiped and served the creation rather than the Creator, who is blessed forever! Amen.

-Romans 1:25

If the idea of globalist leaders with genocidal motivations is too much for you, consider the following quotes from these leading Eugenicists as compiled by SDR Media (https://sdrmedia.wordpress.com/2018/10/28/human-depopulation-quotes/). All of the murderous nonsense to follow is predicated on the myth that there are too many people for the Earth's meager resources to sustain, which is patently false.

1. UK Television Presenter Sir David Attenborough: "We are a plague on the Earth. It's coming home to roost over the next 50 years or so. It's not just climate change; it's sheer space, places to grow food for this enormous horde. Either we limit our population growth or the natural world will do it for us, and the natural world is doing it for us right now"

2. Paul Ehrlich, a former science adviser to President George W. Bush and the author of "The Population Bomb": "To our minds, the fundamental cure, reducing the scale of the human enterprise (including the size of the population) to keep its aggregate consumption within the carrying capacity of Earth is obvious but too much neglected or denied"

3. Paul Ehrlich again, this time on the size of families: "Nobody, in my view, has the right to have 12 children or even three unless the second pregnancy is twins"

4. Dave Foreman, the co-founder of Earth First: "We humans have become a disease, the Humanpox."

5. CNN Founder Ted Turner: "A total world population of 250-300 million people, a 95% decline from present levels, would be ideal."

6. Japan's Deputy Prime Minister Taro Aso about medical patients with serious illnesses: "You cannot sleep well when you think it's all paid by the government. This won't be solved unless you let them hurry up and die."

7. David Rockefeller: "The negative impact of population growth on all of our planetary ecosystems is becoming appallingly evident."

8. Environmental activist Roger Martin: "On a finite planet, the optimum population providing the best quality of life for all, is clearly much smaller than the maximum, permitting bare survival. The more we are, the less for each; fewer people mean better lives."

9. HBO personality Bill Maher: "I'm pro-choice, I'm for assisted suicide, I'm for regular suicide, I'm for whatever gets the freeway moving – that's what I'm for. It's too crowded, the planet is too crowded and we need to promote death."

10. MIT professor Penny Chisholm: "The real trick is, in terms of trying to level off at someplace lower than that 9 billion, is to get the birthrates in the developing countries to drop as fast as we can. And that will determine the level at which humans will level off on earth."

11. Julia Whitty, a columnist for Mother Jones: "The only known solution to ecological overshoot is to decelerate our population growth faster than it's decelerating now and eventually reverse it—at the same time we slow and eventually reverse the rate at which we consume the planet's resources. Success in these twin endeavors will crack our most pressing global issues: climate change, food scarcity,

water supplies, immigration, health care, biodiversity loss, even war. On one front, we've already made unprecedented strides, reducing global fertility from an average 4.92 children per woman in 1950 to 2.56 today—an accomplishment of trial and sometimes brutally coercive error, but also a result of one woman at a time making her individual choices. The speed of this childbearing revolution, swimming hard against biological programming, rates as perhaps our greatest collective feat to date."

12. Colorado State University Professor Philip Cafaro in a paper entitled "Climate Ethics and Population Policy": "Ending human population growth is almost certainly a necessary (but not sufficient) condition for preventing catastrophic global climate change. Indeed, significantly reducing current human numbers may be necessary in order to do so."

13. Professor of Biology at the University of Texas at Austin Eric R. Pianka: "I do not bear any ill will toward people. However, I am convinced that the world, including all humanity, WOULD clearly be much better off without so many of us."

14. Detroit News Columnist Nolan Finley: "Since the national attention is on birth control, here's my idea: If we want to fight poverty, reduce violent crime and bring down our embarrassing drop-out rate, we should swap contraceptives for fluoride in Michigan's drinking water.

We've got a baby problem in Michigan. Too many babies are born to immature parents who don't have the skills to raise them, too many are delivered by poor women who can't afford them, and too many are fathered by sorry layabouts who spread their seed like dandelions and then wander away from the consequences."

15. John Guillebaud, professor of family planning at University College London: "The effect on the planet of

having one child less is an order of magnitude greater than all these other things we might do, such as switching off lights. An extra child is the equivalent of a lot of flights across the planet."

16. Democrat strategist Steven Rattner: "WE need death panels. Well, maybe not death panels, exactly, but unless we start allocating health care resources more prudently — rationing, by its proper name — the exploding cost of Medicare will swamp the federal budget."

17. Matthew Yglesias, a business and economics correspondent for Slate, in an article entitled "The Case for Death Panels, in One Chart": "But not only is this health care spending on the elderly the key issue in the federal budget, our disproportionate allocation of health care dollars to old people surely accounts for the remarkable lack of apparent cost effectiveness of the American health care system. When the patient is already over 80, the simple fact of the matter is that no amount of treatment is going to work miracles in terms of life expectancy or quality of life."

18. Planned Parenthood Founder Margaret Sanger: "All of our problems are the result of overbreeding among the working class"

19. U.S. Supreme Court Justice Ruth Bader Ginsburg: "Frankly I had thought that at the time Roe was decided, there was concern about population growth and particularly growth in populations that we don't want to have too many of."

20. Planned Parenthood Founder Margaret Sanger: "The most merciful thing that the large family does to one of its infant members is to kill it."

21. Salon columnist Mary Elizabeth Williams in an article entitled "So What If Abortion Ends Life?": "All life is not equal. That's a difficult thing for liberals like me to talk about, lest we wind up looking like death-panel-loving, kill-your-grandma-and-your-precious-baby storm troopers. Yet a fetus

can be a human life without having the same rights as the woman in whose body it resides."

22. Alberto Giubilini of Monash University in Melbourne, Australia and Francesca Minerva of the University of Melbournein a paper published in the Journal of Medical Ethics: "[W]hen circumstances occur after birth such that they would have justified abortion, what we call after-birth abortion should be permissible. ... [W]e propose to call this practice 'after-birth abortion', rather than 'infanticide,' to emphasize that the moral status of the individual killed is comparable with that of a fetus ... rather than to that of a child. Therefore, we claim that killing a newborn could be ethically permissible in all the circumstances where abortion would be. Such circumstances include cases where the newborn has the potential to have an (at least) acceptable life, but the well-being of the family is at risk."

23. Nina Fedoroff, a key adviser to Hillary Clinton: "We need to continue to decrease the growth rate of the global population; the planet can't support many more people."

24. Barack Obama's primary science adviser, John P. Holdren: "A program of sterilizing women after their second or third child, despite the relatively greater difficulty of the operation than vasectomy, might be easier to implement than trying to sterilize men.

The development of a long-term sterilizing capsule that could be implanted under the skin and removed when pregnancy is desired opens additional possibilities for coercive fertility control. The capsule could be implanted at puberty and might be removable, with official permission, for a limited number of births."

25. David Brower, the first Executive Director of the Sierra Club: "Childbearing [should be] a punishable crime against society, unless the parents hold a government license ... All potential parents [should be] required to use contraceptive

chemicals, the government issuing antidotes to citizens chosen for childbearing."

26. Thomas Ferguson, former official in the U.S. State Department Office of Population Affairs: "There is a single theme behind all our work–we must reduce population levels. Either governments do it our way, through nice clean methods, or they will get the kinds of mess that we have in El Salvador, or in Iran or in Beirut. Population is a political problem. Once population is out of control, it requires authoritarian government, even fascism, to reduce it..."

27. Mikhail Gorbachev: "We must speak more clearly about sexuality, contraception, about abortion, about values that control population, because the ecological crisis, in short, is the population crisis. Cut the population by 90% and there aren't enough people left to do a great deal of ecological damage."

28. Jacques Costeau: "In order to stabilize world population, we must eliminate 350,000 people per day. It is a horrible thing to say, but it is just as bad not to say it."

29. Finnish environmentalist Pentti Linkola: "If there were a button I could press, I would sacrifice myself without hesitating if it meant millions of people would die"

30. Prince Phillip, husband of Queen Elizabeth II and co-founder of the World Wildlife Fund: "In the event that I am reincarnated, I would like to return as a deadly virus, in order to contribute something to solve overpopulation."

Notice how many of those are environmentalist fanatics. Druids. Earth worshippers. Satanists. As we will see later, the CDC proposes that people be forced into camps against their will. These camps will be called "Green Zones". Why? Because these are Cultist environmentalists that equate human destruction with the revitalization of nature. The entire premise of climate change alarmism is that humans are a disease to the planet. Never mind there being no adequate objective evidence for this. It's just what the people must be told in order for them to accept widespread murder. The people must be fearful. They must believe their very lives are in danger. Once they do, they will gladly relinquish all of their rights and liberties as ordered by their authoritarian leaders. The sheep will cheer all resisters to the gallows because anyone resisting these tyrannical dictates will be viewed as a threat to the very lives of the sheep. We've already seen shadows of this during the COVID-19 pandemic.

My intent here is not to provide a full history of secret societies or Malthusian philosophy, but rather to demonstrate that there is intent and organization behind the movement toward globalization and that depopulation is a precursor to that ultimate agenda. I hope to achieve this not by offering my opinions (though there will be those as well), but by presenting the reader with the Globalist framework via their own documentation, something tangible that leaves little room for debate. Each document discussed can be easily located and confirmed by searching the title online. I have compiled these (and more that are not included in this book) at NWOdocuments.com for convenience of access.

I encourage any curious researchers to read these documents in full, but for those less inclined to designate so much valuable time to such a monotonous task, I have written synopses of each document in this handbook and included quotes with page numbers for easy reference and verification. In this age of deception and propaganda, one can't be too careful. I encourage the reader to fact-check every quotation.

To provide further commentary, the second portion of this book consists of newsletters that I send out to those who subscribe to my website as they may assist the reader in some of the real-world application of this material.

I considered including a full synopsis of Schwab's Great Reset in this book, but that would open it up for his Fourth

Industrial Revolution book as well, and Aldous Huxley and Albert Pike and every other secret society alumni who authored a book involving the NWO, so I've limited this book to only a handful of their documents that bear relevancy to current events. That said, I will offer a very brief synopsis of The Great Reset since I reference it throughout this book somewhat regularly.

The central thrust of Schwab's book can be summarized as such: COVID-19 presents an opportunity for us to "build back better" – especially in terms of clean energy, digital currency, global interdependence, and equity. He cites nationalism and failure to obey government dictates as primary barriers to achieving this new world made possible by COVID-19, the blessing in disguise.

Schwab begins the book by attempting to normalize draconian economy-shattering lockdowns, citing a history of plagues from times past. "Thus, there is nothing new about the confinement and lockdowns imposed upon much of the world to manage COVID-19" (p. 13). Schwab further states that "the authorities that try to keep us safe by enforcing confinement measures are often perceived as agents of oppression."

Yes, Schwab. That's because that is what they are. When I'm watching a woman being dragged from her home and jailed for speaking out against the state-sanctioned COVID narrative, I am watching oppression. When I am seeing governments attempting to enforce limitations on family gatherings during Thanksgiving, I am watching oppression. Forcing small businesses to close while allowing Walmart and Target to remain open is oppression. Only the monopolies shall survive. The free market must be decimated in order to make way for the New World Order! The Great Reset uses climate change, COVID-19, and any other excuse at hand to justify the implementation of a New World Order.

Of all tyrannies, a tyranny sincerely exercised for the good of its victims may be the most oppressive.

-C.S. Lewis

Why would a subversive cabal openly publish their plans if their motivations were nefarious? It's a reasonable question. I would ask the same about clearly unconstitutional bills being openly proposed by legislation. These secret societies are relegated to underground functions because the free world patently rejects their morally defunct philosophies and objectives, yet they can achieve nothing without our complicity. If they were to continue plotting behind the scenes, they would likely be found out and subsequently destroyed, therefore it is better to operate in plain sight by disguising their motivations as philanthropic endeavors to achieve world peace and save the planet. Then if anyone accuses them of doing what they are actually doing, they can plausibly deny any accusation. At the top of the pyramid, their true objectives are discussed away from public view, such as at private Bilderberg meetings. This is where they would openly acknowledge an objective such as destroying the Western economy for example, though the plan they would present to their underlings as well as to the public might sound more like, "we need to promote green energy to save the planet". The result is the same. They still get their economic destruction (which is about all green policies are good for) even while positioning themselves as benevolent, selfless heroes. Plausible deniability. It's how they get away with everything. You've likely seen it yourself as politicians brazenly, confidently lie in congressional hearings almost always without consequence. They hide in plain sight and call themselves philanthropists. If you're them, it's the most logical approach.

No matter how paranoid or conspiracy-minded you are, what the government is actually doing is worse than you imagine.

- William Blum, Investigative Journalist

The World Population Plan of Action

Kopf

UNITED NATIONS POPULATION INFORMATION NETWORK (POPIN)
UN Population Division, Department of Economic and Social Affairs,
with support from the UN Population Fund (UNFPA)

World Population Plan of Action

The electronic version of this document is being made available by
the United Nations Population Information Network (POPIN) Gopher of
the Population Division, Department for Economic and Social
Information and Policy Analysis.

****

WORLD POPULATION PLAN OF ACTION

The World Population Conference,

Having due regard for human aspirations for a better quality
of life and for rapid socio-economic development,

Taking into consideration the interrelationship between
population situations and socio-economic development,

Decides on the following World Population Plan of Action as
a policy instrument within the broader context of the
internationally adopted strategies for national and international
progress:

From August 19th to 30th in 1974, representatives from 135 countries met in Bucharest, Romania to discuss the detriment of the human population on the healthy functioning of nations. This gave birth to the United Nations' World Population Plan of Action.

The title speaks for itself. The World Population Plan of Action is a document created by the United Nations Population Information Network (POPIN) arguing that there are too many people on the planet and something needs to be done about it. It should be noted that in the United States' follow-up version of the UN's World Population Plan of Action, they admit that they have no idea what population the Earth can actually sustain. I have heard it said that the entire population of the world could live comfortably within Alaska alone, and the resources necessary for the survival of mankind are all renewable, therefore, there is no problem of overpopulation. It is yet another lie coming from globalist overlords, just as the great global warming hoax. Note that all of the existential threats being propagated against us are invisible, that is, we only "know" they're a threat because that is what we are told, though we have not observed them for ourselves. And not surprisingly, the only solution for all of these invisible threats just so happens to be the widespread removal of our individual human liberties. They had used different versions of the same threats years ago as we will see in the NSSM-200 document which warns of an impending ice age! Now it's the opposite. And the polar ice caps are supposed to have melted by now according to their projections years ago, and our coastal cities are all supposed to be submerged under the ocean even though some of the very people making those claims then went on to purchase oceanfront properties proving they don't actually believe what they warn you about, they just need *you* to believe it. The Green Movement is a huge money maker and as long as fearful people continue to buy into the propaganda, the propagandists can continue to buy their oceanfront properties.

This is a classic Hegelian Dialectic – a strategy utilized by governments wherein there is a "solution" they wish to impose (generally resulting in the removal of the rights of the people) so they create the problem in order to justify their solution to the people. For example, "Our deepest apologies for force-vaccinating you (making us rich beyond comprehension) and creating a system of medical authoritarianism, but we had to do it because of this pandemic (that we created)". It's simple and it works. That is why they do it over and over and over again.

With that in mind, let's take a look at the Cloward-Piven strategy as there is no time in modern history that it has ever been more relevant than now. This is a strategy proposed in 1966 by Columbia University sociologists Richard Andrew Cloward and Frances Fox Piven that seeks to destroy the West by creating a crisis that fosters increasing dependence on the government. You'll notice that the tenets of the strategy are currently underway:

1. Overload and Break the Welfare System
2. Have Chaos Ensue
3. Take Control in the Chaos
4. Implement Socialism and Communism through Government Force

Cloward and Piven were Marxists riding the coattails of Saul Alinsky, hero of Hillary Clinton. Alinsky wrote "Rules for Radicals", a Socialist playbook that authoritarians absolutely adore. Not surprisingly, the book actually opens with a dedication to Lucifer. Alinsky's 8 commandments for creating a tyrannical social state are as follows. The first is the most important.

1) **Healthcare**– Control healthcare and you control the people.
2) **Poverty** – Increase the Poverty level as high as possible, poor people are easier to control and will not fight back if you

are providing everything for them to live.

3) **Debt** – Increase the debt to an unsustainable level. That way you are able to increase taxes, and this will produce more poverty.

4) **Gun Control**– Remove the ability to defend themselves from the Government. That way you are able to create a police state.

5) **Welfare** – Take control of every aspect of their lives (Food, Housing, and Income)

6) **Education** – Take control of what people read and listen to – take control of what children learn in school.

7) **Religion** – Remove the belief in the God from the Government and schools.

8) **Class Warfare** – Divide the people into the wealthy and the poor. This will cause more discontent and it will be easier to take (tax) the wealthy with the support of the poor.

All of these are currently operational. Anyone arguing that there is no plot to take down the West will have an extremely difficult time of it when everything we see occurring today is straight out of their playbook. Whether or not we'd like to be, we are a part of what will likely become the worst period in human history. Destroying the West is absolutely crucial for the globalist depopulation plan. This plan was in existence prior to the UN's World Population Plan of Action, however, it is an appropriate document to begin with.

The authors will not come out and say that humans should be murdered, but with some careful reading between the lines, one can see that they are setting the stage for it. Note the references to a new world order. Also note that many of the things that we have always considered civil rights issues are actually part of the depopulation agenda, i.e., the heavy focus on women's empowerment. They don't care whether women are empowered, they just want to convince women that they are oppressed by traditional roles and foster a desire within them to leave the home to work so that they produce fewer children. I'm not making an argument against civil liberties. I am saying *their* motivation for taking up social justice causes is not for consideration of the individual, but to reduce "fertility" as they phrase it.

On page 2 we immediately see who is behind this work as it states, "The Declaration on the Establishment of a *New International Economic Order* and the Programme of Action to achieve it, adopted by the United Nations General Assembly at its sixth special session (resolutions 3201 (S-VI) and 3202 (S-VI) of 1 May 1974), provide the most recent overall framework for international cooperation."

On page 7, we see a thinly veiled lament about all the senior citizens that are allowed to live and adversely impact the economy: "...the population 65 years and over is expected to increase by 3.5 per cent a year. Not only are the numbers and proportions of the aged increasing rapidly but the social and economic conditions which face them are also rapidly changing."

In 1798, Thomas Robert Malthus wrote *An Essay on the Principle of Population* which gave rise to an economic philosophy known now as Malthusianism, which essentially proposes an inverse relationship between a healthy economy and a rising population. Basically, the more people there are, the less wealth there is to go around, thus the need for keeping the human population in check.

One hears echoes of Malthus throughout the World Population Plan of Action as it is continually implied that economic growth must be synonymous with population reduction. On page 8 we read, "Efforts made by developing countries to speed up economic growth must be viewed by the entire international community as a global endeavor to improve the quality of life for all people of the world, supported by a just utilization of the world's wealth, resources and technology in the spirit of the new international economic order. It also demonstrates that countries wishing to affect their population growth must anticipate future demographic trends and take appropriate decisions and actions in their plans for economic and social development well in advance."

Part C on page 12 states that one of the principles of the plan is "to promote socio-economic measures and programmes whose aim is to affect, inter alia, population growth, morbidity and mortality, reproduction and family formation...". The reader may notice that the language used throughout this plan is vague. They write that their aim is to affect population growth, mortality, and reproduction, but never quite muster the courage to clarify in what way they mean. Of course in a document centered on managing the human population, it is easy to assume in what way they mean to "affect" mortality and reproduction.

Another principle listed at the top of page 13 is "to promote the status of women and the expansion of their roles... and the creation of awareness among all women of their current and potential roles in national life." One may interpret this as, "We will instill dissatisfaction among women and convince them that slaving their lives away at a job they hate is actually freedom, and being a full time mother and homemaker is a form of oppression." Perhaps the reader at this point views my rephrasing here as quite a leap in logic, however, you will see a good deal more of this kind of rhetoric as you continue reading, and at some point it becomes evident that feminism as a social movement was a psychological operation installed by the leaders of nations in an effort to keep the human population to a minimum.

See if you notice anything curious about this statement on page 15: "The short-term effect of mortality reduction on population growth rates is symptomatic of the early development process and must be viewed as beneficial. Sustained reductions in fertility have generally been preceded by reductions in mortality. Although this relationship is complex, mortality reduction may be a prerequisite to a decline in fertility."

Translation: "Although we don't want people live, their continued existence is a sign that fewer babies are likely to be born in the near future according to our data, so it is beneficial at least in that regard." Likewise, when reductions in infant and child mortality are spoken of favorably, it is only because when people's children have a higher probability of survival, they are less likely to intentionally procreate a large family.

Page 20 promotes "a more equitable distribution of income, land, social services and amenities," as well as the importance of indoctrination: "It is recommended that Governments consider making provision, in both their formal and non-formal educational programmes for informing their people of the consequences of existing or alternative fertility behavior for the well-being of the family, for educational and psychological development of children...". One must wonder to what *non-formal* educational programs they are referring. As the reader continues through this book, the blatant promotion of propaganda will become increasingly evident. It is an extremely necessary element of the New World Order agenda.

Page 21: "In the light of the principles of this Plan of Action, countries which consider their birth-rates detrimental to their national purposes are invited to consider setting quantitative goals and implementing policies that may lead to the attainment of such goals by 1985. Nothing herein should interfere with the sovereignty of any Government to adopt or not to adopt such quantitative goals."

Quantitative goals? At least they haven't begun speaking about qualitative goals. Yet. The final sentence of that paragraph might be interpreted as a promise to all nations that should their governments wish to implement more extreme measures to achieve a reduction in birth rates, the UN will be happy not to interfere (or perhaps look the other way when necessary).

Page 23: "Improvement of the status of women in the family and in society can contribute, where desired, to smaller family sizes and the opportunity for women to plan births also improves their individual status."

Page 25: "Governments should take into account not only short-term economic returns or alternative patterns but also the social and environmental costs and benefits involved as well as equity and social justice in the distribution of the benefits of development among all groups and regions."

Even decades ago our virtue-signaling governments were opportunistically hijacking social movements and fostering a sense of oppression among key groups in an effort to weaponize their sentiments against the proliferation of humanity. Of course, that much should be obvious. Surely there are no people who still believe our governments have righteous motivations or seek the welfare of their people.

Speaking of motivation, page 36 emphasizes the need for further study and research into the "means for understanding and improving the motivations of people to participate in the formulation and implementation of population programmes." In other words, it is important that they learn how to "properly motivate" (brainwash) people into getting on board with population programs. It isn't hard to see today how far they've come since 1974. Their fear campaigns, such as that of climate change alarmism, have become mainstream. It's another Hegelian dialectic. *Watch out! The world will end because there are too many people!* They propose a problem that doesn't actually exist so they can implement their solution to depopulate, and people believe their alarmism because they've been made comfortable with the control mechanisms of modern bread and circus such as sporting events and junk food. Such people are too committed to their easy lifestyle to dare challenge the status quo. On a subconscious level they are shouting like spoiled children, *I'll bury my head in the sand until I suffocate if I have to!* Desperate to maintain their comfortable delusions.

Also an area of study the UN would like to expand on is "the interrelationships among patterns of family formation, nutrition and health, reproductive biology, and the incidence, causes, and treatment of sterility" as stated on page 37. Let's employ a bit of logic here. When a document focused on human depopulation is advocating for the study of how to treat sterility, is it because they want to actually treat sterility or is it because they want to learn the mechanisms that influence sterility so they can use them to decrease fertility?

Further down the page, they hint at their war on the family unit, specifically targeting women for propaganda, and again promoting further research into male and female fertility. Hopefully the reader is beginning to get a better feel for the double speak employed by these subtle tyrants.

Let's interpret this line from page 40: "efforts should be made to eradicate illiteracy, to promote education among the youth and abolish factors discriminating against women." Their data indicates that poor people reproduce more, hence their apparently benevolent desire to help people become literate (and therefore more likely to secure more gainful employment, thereby reproducing less). To promote education among the youth simply means to indoctrinate them against the idea of finding large families, or any family, desirable. And of course the never-ending feigned concern for women – we know what that's about by now.

Further down on page 40, it reads, "Governments are invited to use all available means for disseminating population information." Here they are dressing up their advocacy for an aggressive propaganda campaign in a more covert tone.

Concerning the tone of the World Population Plan of Action, I conclude that it is indirect so as to be more palatable to the various nations they are selling their Malthusian ideals to. One may argue that my interpretation of their motivation for wanting poor people to be literate or women to be employed is grossly misguided, but my interpretation of the language used is informed by the WPPOA's sister document, the NSSM-200, which communicates more overtly as it enjoyed the privilege of having been a classified document.

Kopf

NSSM-200

(National Security Study Memorandum 200)

Implications of Worldwide Population Growth For U.S. Security and Overseas Interests

National Security Study Memorandum

NSSM 200

Implications of Worldwide Population Growth
For U.S. Security and Overseas Interests
(THE KISSINGER REPORT)

December 10, 1974

CLASSIFIED BY Harry C. Blaney, III
SUBJECT TO GENERAL DECLASSIFICATION SCHEDULE
OF EXECUTIVE ORDER 11652 AUTOMATICALLY DOWN-
GRADED AT TWO YEAR INTERVALS AND DECLASSIFIED
ON DECEMBER 31, 1980.

This document can only be declassified by the White House.

From 1969 to 1974, 206 National Security Study Memoranda were issued under the Nixon Administration as formal directives to study issues relating to national security and foreign policy. The 200th NSSM was commissioned to explore the dangers of overpopulation especially as it relates to the exploitation of other countries' resources. Note that the NSSM-200 is alternately referred to as "The Kissinger Report" as in the Henry Kissinger who says things like, "He who controls the food controls the people".

The NSSM-200 offers this criticism of the WPPOA: "The World Population Plan of Action, despite its wordiness and often hesitant tone, contains all the necessary provisions for effective population growth control programs at national and international levels. It lacks only plain statements of quantitative goals with time frames for their accomplishment (p.71)."

Indeed the tone of the NSSM-200 includes more "plain statements", though never so plain as to openly advocate for genocide (however, anyone actually reading the document can decipher what they are saying without saying as I will demonstrate). Even in a temporarily classified document like the NSSM-200 at least *some* discretion must be exercised if a majority of stakeholders are to adopt such a nefarious plan.

The Malthusian premise is made clear on page 6: "Rapid population growth creates a severe drag on rates of economic development", and further down the page, "Adverse economic factors which generally result from rapid population growth include the concentration of developmental resources on increasing food production to ensure survival for a larger population rather than on improving living conditions for smaller total numbers." In short, more people means less wealth, the subtext of course being that the haves must thin the numbers of the have-nots so the haves can have even more.

On page 7 the authors acknowledge that "the interrelationships between development and population growth are complex and not wholly understood." So they don't know much about it, but they know enough to conclude that there needs to be fewer humans. Here they specify some of the ways they intend to achieve this population reduction:

1) Improved health care and nutrition to reduce child mortality. This is not because they want children to live. Remember that the World Population Plan of Action encouraged the reader not to be dismayed by humans not dying, that human survival is only symptomatic of an oncoming population decrease.

2) Education and improved social status for women. This is not because they care about you or your daughter or you mother, but rather because educated/indoctrinated women tend to reproduce less.

3) Increased female employment. Same motivation.

4) Improved old-age security. Not because they want the elderly to be cared for, but because it removes one of the primary motivators for reproduction (to be cared for in old age).

5) Assistance for the rural poor (who generally have the highest fertility) with actions to redistribute income and resources including providing privately owned farms. Not because they care for the impoverished, but because it is the demographic with the highest fertility rate, which is unacceptable.

In the NSSM-200, "Family planning" is a euphemism for abortion which they consistently praise for its efficacy in human eradication. On page 10, it states, "Family planning information and materials based on present technology should be made fully available as rapidly as possible to the 85% of the populations in key LDCs not now reached, essentially rural poor who have the highest fertility." Whether they are getting rid of poor people by redistributing wealth to them or aborting them, it makes no difference just so long as something is done about it.

Page 11 reiterates "creating conditions conducive to fertility decline" which as previously stated includes, "developing alternatives to children as a source of old age security" and "education of new generations on the desirability of smaller families" (indoctrinate children).

Allow me to present a question. Is a guilty party or innocent party more inclined to be overly concerned with ensuring they appear harmless to others? Several times throughout the document, the authors emphasize the importance of not appearing to have malicious intent as on page 13: "We must take care that our activities should not give the appearance to the LDCs of an industrialized country policy directed against the LDCs," and further down on the same page, "To help assure others of our intentions, we should indicate our emphasis on the right of individuals…".

On the next page just after promoting more "family planning", they "recommend increased emphasis on mass media" (propaganda) to further achieve their aims. But the most poignant statements on this page involve food control, stating that "even stronger measures are required and some fundamental *very difficult moral issues* need to be addressed. These include, for example, our own consumption patterns, *mandatory programs, tight control of our food resources* (emphasis added by this writer)." This coming from 'control-the-food-control-the-people' Kissinger in a document about population management.

Page 20: "With the beginnings of the industrial revolution and of modern medicine over two hundred years ago, population growth rates accelerated." This statement seems to lay the foundation for the motivation to usurp the medical industry to decrease the population, which is currently occurring as I write these words. Legislation has been recently passed in certain states and countries that enforces a particular medical narrative, whether supported by evidence or not. We are now witnessing the inception of a medical dictatorship. Medicine that contributes to human longevity has been identified as a problem as evidenced by the statement on page 20.

Another problem is stated on the following page: "The typical developing country has 41% to 45% of its population under 15. This means that a tremendous amount of future parents, compared to existing parents, are already born." There is a dehumanizing implication to referring to children as "future parents". This should come as no surprise as the architects of the New World Order are intrinsically anti-human. If the reader has not yet drawn that conclusion, keep reading. Further down the page, the authors breathe a sigh of relief that "famine pestilence, war, or birth control" will ensure the population does not get too out of control. One might wonder why our world leaders wouldn't play an active role in fomenting famine, pestilence, and war (all currently in process) since those things are such blessings to their Mother Earth, Gaia, who thirsts for human blood. Why not? After all, they do seem to endorse "difficult moral choices" and draconian measures: "short of Draconian measures there is no possibility that any LDC can stabilize its population at less than double its present size" (p. 28).

Prepare to roll your eyes. Page 36 states, "Climatic changes are poorly understood, but a persistent atmospheric cooling trend since 1940 has been established." This is discussed in the context of possible famine. 'Science' told us in the 1970s that we'd be freezing and starving to death in an ice age by today, now it tells us that the ice caps will melt, the polar bears will die, and coastal cities will flood. This was supposed to have come to pass decades ago, yet the ice caps are as icy as ever, the polar bear population is increasing (perhaps they could use some family planning), and our fear-mongering politicians continue to buy ocean-front properties because they are of course not at all under water.

Why do they persist with their climate change alarmism despite the glaring fact that they are consistently wrong? Because it is perfect problem-reaction-solution Hegelian dialectic fodder. The ever-invisible threat. The people cannot perceive the climate changing at the imperceptible rate they claim it is, therefore, they simply must take the scientific political overlords at their word. They'd never lead us astray, they want what is best for us.

An invisible problem in the problem-reaction-solution formula for control is the best kind of problem for it is conveniently unfalsifiable. This formula is the modus operandi of the New World Order operatives. And speaking of the NWO, the next page (37) states that stifling the growth rates of the Less Developed Countries would "improve the possibilities for long-term development and integration into a peaceful world order." Furthermore, exploiting poor countries (which remember they must make great efforts to not appear malicious to) for their resources is also an important step toward this "world order" they continually fantasize about. Page 40 states, "The real problems of mineral supplies lie not in basic physical sufficiency, but in the politico-economic issues of access, terms for exploration and exploitation, and division of the benefits among producers, consumers, and host country governments."

Eugenics is the practice of selecting favorable genetic traits in an effort to produce the ideal human. In ancient

Sparta, children that were born with genetic flaws were murdered. An example of a more modern eugenicist is Adolph Hitler. It should come as no surprise that a depopulation plan includes a eugenic motivation as evidenced on page 51 where "child quality versus quantity" is discussed.

The following quotation provides a good summary of the fact that many of the good things we enjoy in America are only allowed because they contribute something to suppressing the population level: "Such selective policies would focus on improved health care and nutrition directed toward reduced infant and child mortality, universal schooling and adult literacy, especially for women, increasing the legal age for marriage, greater opportunities for female employment in the money economy, improved old-age social security arrangements, and agricultural modernization focused on small farmers (p.53)."

Remember, the plan is to kill children in utero. Those that survive and are born should be kept healthy only because parents have less children when they are more apt to survive. Providing for the elderly is only done to remove the primary motivation for people to have large families: to be cared for by their children when they grow old. Don't be fooled by their appearance of benevolence, which remember, they take great care to present themselves as. On page 92 they offer a concise statement that speaks to the motivation for their seemingly good-natured goal of reducing poverty: "The desire for large families diminishes as income rises." They do not wish anyone to be wealthy, just wealthy enough not to reproduce.

Referring to the population of Bangladesh on page 62, the authors seem to advocate for death a disease: "The present 75 million or so, unless slowed by famine, disease, or massive birth control, will double in 23 years and exceed 170 million by 2000."

One should find their projections difficult to take seriously when the year is 2023 at the time of this writing and we are not in the middle of an ice age, nor are our coastal cities flooded or our forests all aflame. Of course we are decades past the year 2000 and the population of Bangladesh still has not reached 170 million. Though with every passing year we may be getting closer to the "future world order" (p. 63) that these psychopathic liars continue to prognosticate about.

Despite the tendency toward embellishment and outright dishonesty, the authors accidentally tell the truth on page 74 and admit that they really have no clue how many people the world can sustain: "...nor can we state with assurance the limits of the world's ecological carrying capacity." In that case, this whole memorandum is a waste of time and the overpopulation crisis is as much a mythology as the climate crisis.

Page 75 lists the countries that should take priority due to being the fastest developing at the time: India, Bangladesh, Pakistan, Nigeria, Mexico, Indonesia, Brazil, The Philippines, Thailand, Egypt, Turkey, Ethiopia, and Colombia. On page 77 they expand, "Specific country strategies must be worked out for each of the highest priority countries and for the lower priority ones. These strategies will take account of such factors as: national attitudes and sensitivities on family planning; which instruments will be most acceptable, opportunities for effective use of assistance, and need of external capital or operating assistance." And as usual, further down the page, "In these sensitive relationships, however, it is important in style as well as substance to avoid the appearance of coercion."

On page 79 it is recommended to give "high priority to experimentation and pilot projects." Salinas is an isolated village in the Dominican Republic where all the babies are born female. Those who are actually biologically male do not develop male sex organs until they reach puberty. One may wonder how such a phenomenon could impact one isolated village, yet outside the village the phenomenon ceases to occur. We know from the NSSM-200 that our government is heavily invested in studying reproduction, fertility, and giving "high priority to experimentation." If I lived in Salinas, I would stop drinking the water.

Page 80 emphasizes the need for "concentrating on the education and indoctrination of the rising generation of children regarding the desirability of smaller family size." Do you see the effects of this indoctrination today? Do you discern that note of disdain for those with large families as evidenced by such remarks as, "she needs to close her legs" or "he needs to keep it in his pants"?

Also on page 80 we see a plug for improved food security: "Without improved food security there will be pressure leading to possible conflict and the desire for large families for 'insurance' purposes, thus undermining other development and population control efforts." Recall their previous statements regarding food control, suggesting "difficult moral choices" may be necessary. By food security, do they mean bread lines? A document that explores how to lower the human population while discussing controlling the food supply is a little unsettling.

On page 83, several questions are posed:

- Should the US set even higher agricultural production goals which would enable it to provide additional major food resources to other countries? Should they be nationally or internationally controlled?

- On what basis should such food resources then be provided? Would food be considered an instrument of national power? Will we be forced to make choices as to whom we can reasonably assist, and if so, should population efforts be a criterion for such assistance?

- Is the US prepared to accept food rationing to help people who can't/won't control their population growth?

- Should the US seek to change its own food consumption patterns toward more efficient uses of protein?

- Are mandatory population control measure appropriate for the US and/or for others?

Page 85: "Moreover, with assistance from AID a number of private family planning organizations (e.g., Pathfinder Fund, International Planned Parenthood Foundation, Population Council) have significantly expanded their worldwide population programs." Here we have in an official government document an admission that Planned Parenthood has little to do with women's rights but is rather a depopulation program.

Other depopulation programs are referred to on page 93: "Similarly, there have been some controversial, but remarkably successful, experiments in India in which financial incentives, along with other motivational devices, were used to get large numbers of men to accept vasectomies." Further experimentation is recommended on page 94: "AID should encourage other donors in LDC governments to carry out parallel strategies of research, experimentation, and (cost-effective well-evaluated) large-scale operations programs on factors affecting fertility." And on page 95: "These programs should, where feasible, include curricula to motivate the next generation toward a two-child family." Page 96 emphasizes again the need to "experiment on a large scale with innovative ways of tackling the outstanding problems."

As a long-term approach, a safe and effective injectable (where have we heard that before?) contraceptive is recommended on page 110: "an effective and safe male contraceptive is needed, in particular an injection which will be effective for specified periods of time." One may want to pay attention to the birth rate in this age of mass coerced injection.

Of all population control mechanisms, abortion is the gold standard. "No country has reduced its population growth without resorting to abortion (p. 83)." These Malthusians have been successful in "avoiding the appearance of coercion" because they are crafty: "Family planning in the health context shows a concern for the well-being of the family (p. 112)." People now feel so righteously about their right to kill their unborn 'future parents' that they will march on DC for it, and thus it has become the most ubiquitous self-imposed depopulation strategy in the world. "Indeed, abortion, legal and illegal, now has become the most widespread fertility control method in use in the world today (p. 115)."

Near the end of the document on page 117 there is discussion of the best methodology for disseminating propaganda to indoctrinate the impressionable masses: "A.I.D.'s work suggests that radio, posters, printed material, and various types of personal contacts by health/family planning workers tend to be more cost-effective than television except in those areas (generally urban) where a TV system is already in place" – bear in mind this document is from 1974 – "which reaches more than just the middle and upper classes. There is a great scope for use of mass media, particularly in the initial stages of making people aware of the benefits of family planning and of services available."

Are your beliefs really your own? Have you been programmed to detest the idea of large families? To believe that the world is overpopulated? To think that abortion is a fundamental human right and those who oppose it are misogynistic oppressors? Is your moral code the product of an anti-human government's indoctrination program?

That our government believes there are too many people alive is demonstrable by the existence of their official white papers such as the NSSM-200, and many conclusions can be subsequently drawn from this using basic logic. For instance, if a government believes there are too many people, would it be motivated to preserve the lives of its citizens? One may answer, yes, they are clearly dedicated to reducing infant mortality and enhancing old-age security. But have you been paying attention to the subtext? The barely contained excitement over the possibility of disease and famine? The hints of using starvation as a weapon? Imagine the plain language used in documents that have never been declassified as the NSSM-200 has.

Moving along, we will take a look at what else is on the New World Order's agenda.

Kopf

Agenda 2030

TRANSFORMING OUR WORLD:

THE 2030 AGENDA FOR
SUSTAINABLE DEVELOPMENT

The 70th General Assembly of the United Nations adopted the 2030 agenda for sustainable development on the 25th of September, 2015. I am not including Agenda 21 in this book because Agenda 2030 encompasses it. The title of the agenda is *Transforming Our World*. It's almost as if they are seeking to establish a New World Order, or Great Reset, under the guise of sustainable development.

Because the authors are fully aware that this agenda requires the demolition of nations (in order to "build them back better" of course) and the implementation of tyrannical policies, they are sure to steer the reader's focus away from their own tyranny to the "tyranny of poverty" to justify their objectives. The preamble states, "All countries and all stakeholders, acting in collaborative partnership will implement this plan. We are resolved to free the human race from the tyranny of poverty and want and to heal and secure our planet."

Strangely enough, girl power is a primary component of sustainable development all throughout this document. Yet we know from the WPPOA and NSSM-200 what the true motivation for what is termed "gender equality" really is. According to the preamble, the sustainable development goals "seek to realize the human rights of all and to achieve gender equality and the empowerment of all women and girls". The goals target the following 5 P's:

People: *We are determined to end poverty and hunger, in all their forms and dimensions, and to ensure that all human beings can fulfil their potential in dignity and equality and in a healthy environment.*

I assume they mean to end poverty and hunger in the same manner that their World Population Plan of Action proposes. If there are no people, then there is nobody to be hungry. This smacks of the hypersanitized welfare state depicted in their *Plannedopolous* videos, which the reader can easily view online with a quick search of "Plannedopolous" in your favorite browser.

Planet: *We are determined to protect the planet from degradation, including through sustainable consumption and production, sustainably managing its natural resources and taking urgent action on climate change, so that it can support the needs of the present and future generations.*

Yes, we have seen all the "benefits" of these green policies that seem to succeed only in destroying affordable food, fuel, housing, and anything else one can think of.

Prosperity: *We are determined to ensure that all human beings can enjoy prosperous and fulfilling lives and that economic, social and technological progress occurs in harmony with nature.*

"In harmony with nature" is phrasing taken directly from the Georgia Guidestones which served as the New World Order's monument to human depopulation, advocating for a population of no larger than 500,000,000, which would require a massive die off. You will learn more about the "technological progress" to which they refer as you read further, but for now I will provide a brief foreshadowing – it isn't something any sane human would desire.

Peace: *We are determined to foster peaceful, just and inclusive societies which are free from fear and violence. There can be no sustainable development without peace and no peace without sustainable development.*

"Peaceful, just, and inclusive societies" for whom? We live in an age when truly peace-seeking people are called terrorists and accused of violence by those who ignore actual violence such as that taking place in Chinese death camps. The justice they are referring to is the kind of "justice" that has resulted in elderly women being held prisoner for years simply for being present at the US capitol on January 6th. You will see who Globalist governments consider "violent" or "terroristic" as you read on. Again, I will give you a hint: if you're reading this book, it's probably you.

Partnership: *We are determined to mobilize the means required to implement this Agenda through a revitalised Global Partnership for Sustainable Development, based on a spirit of strengthened global solidarity, focussed in particular on the needs of the poorest and most vulnerable and with the participation of all countries, all stakeholders and all people.*

Of course, there can be no success without partnering (whether by coercion or otherwise) with the most powerful governments and non-governmental organizations such as Amazon, Twitter, Facebook, etc., all of whom are already Globalist-controlled.

Page 3 offers a brief summary of the 2030 sustainability goals: "We resolve, between now and 2030, to end poverty and hunger everywhere; to combat inequalities within and among countries; to build peaceful, just and inclusive societies; to protect human rights and promote gender equality and the empowerment of women and girls; and to ensure the lasting protection of the planet and its natural resources. We resolve also to create conditions for sustainable, inclusive and sustained economic growth, shared prosperity and decent work for all, taking into account different levels of national development and capacities."

Sounds nice, doesn't it? Page 5 reiterates much of the same, identifying gender equality as a "key challenge" along with climate change and reproductive health. All of these are related to the myth of overpopulation. Women's empowerment specifically is heavily focused on: "The systematic mainstreaming of a gender perspective in the implementation of the Agenda is crucial (p.6)." So the most pressing global matters include disease, war, famine, terrorism, death and destruction everywhere… oh, and women's empowerment. The comically disproportionate focus on girl power in these documents makes no sense at all except within the context of the WPPOA and NSSM-200.

There are many lies to unpack in point number 26 on page 7: "To promote physical and mental health and well-being, and to extend life expectancy for all, we must achieve universal health coverage and access to quality health care. No one must be left behind. We commit to accelerating the progress made to date in reducing newborn, child and maternal mortality by ending all such preventable deaths before 2030. We are committed to ensuring universal access to sexual and reproductive health-care services, including for family planning, information and education."

They "promote physical health" by saturating the market with GMO foods that cause all manner of disease and malady (increasing the wealth of their pharmaceutical partners). They "promote mental health" by endorsing mental illness via gender confusion and praising gender dysphoria, which remains a mental illness per the Diagnostic Statistical Manual #5. They hope to extend life expectancy only to deter human reproduction. They promote "access to sexual and reproductive health-care services" only to eradicate as many unborn children as possible.

Under point number 27 on page 8, the authors state that economic prosperity will "only be possible if wealth is shared." Point 28 promotes changing "unsustainable consumption and production patterns", i.e., 'you will have nothing and you will be happy' as stated by the World

Economic Forum. Point 29 promotes open borders: "We will cooperate internationally to ensure safe, orderly and regular migration involving full respect for human rights and the humane treatment of migrants regardless of migration status, of refugees and of displaced persons."

On page 10, sports (bread and circus) are identified as important to the enabling of sustainable development, though they claim it's because they contribute to the promotion of tolerance and respect and the empowerment of women and young people. My suspicion is that this is simply an acknowledgement that sports are an invaluable tool to distract the simple-minded during key movements that may "lend to the appearance of coercion" or be otherwise damaging to the NWO agenda.

The next section on page 10 describes how they will bring together "governments, the private sector, civil society, the United Nations system and other actors" to facilitate the full implementation of their sustainable development goals. It's a team effort made not only by the UN, but by entities influenced by the UN and other powerful globalist actors such as the WEF, WHO, World Bank, Big Tech, Big Pharma, Hollywood, the education system, mainstream media, and so many more. A common argument against the idea that there is a push toward global domination is that there would have to be too many people "in on it" than what is possible. Look at the above list of monumental entities that are "in on it" as a matter of public record. It's not impossible, it's almost inevitable.

On page 15 there is a stated goal to "by 2030, reduce at least by half the proportion of men, women, and children of all ages living in poverty" and further down, "by 2030, end hunger." This is extremely ambitious, but it is a noble endeavor, unless of course depopulation is the means by which they seek to achieve it, which we know from the WPPOA is what they advocate for.

The goals listed on page 16 that they hope to achieve by 2030 include increasing investment in plant and livestock gene banks, end epidemics (by creating COVID-19?), halve the number of global deaths and injuries from road traffic accidents by 2020 (perhaps via lockdowns?), provide vaccines for all, and support the research and development of vaccines.

On page 17, we see the advocacy for indoctrinating students that typifies globalist documents: "By 2030, ensure that all learners acquire the knowledge and skills needed to promote sustainable development, including, among others, through education for sustainable development and sustainable lifestyles, human rights, gender equality, promotion of a culture of peace and non-violence, global citizenship and appreciation of cultural diversity and of culture's contribution to sustainable development." The education system has become nothing more than the indoctrination system of the globalists. Children and naïve college students are now even more inculcated into this ideology than they were before the sustainable development goals were introduced. Perhaps that is to account for the obscene rash of confused fascist activists that never have a clue what they're talking about that we are now unfortunately encountering with increasing frequency.

Page 19 is where you will find their stated goal of ensuring "universal access to affordable, reliable, and modern energy services" by 2030. "Modern energy" is a euphemism for inefficient energy. One need only look to the headlines to see the obvious war on oil, natural gas, and other forms of demonized energy despite the failure to produce any actual evidence that any of it harms the environment. In fact, the "pollutant" CO_2 is pumped into greenhouses to make plants thinker, healthier, and more productive. Strange that one of the primary substances said to be destroying the planet seems to achieve quite the opposite effect.

Of course the real problem with these energies is that they afford freedom to the people. Gasoline or propane can be bought and stored in large quantities by individuals, however, one would be hard-pressed to produce their own electricity in quantities sufficient to power their entire home. Dictators love electricity. It can be turned off with the push of a button. It requires government permission to use. Gas-powered vehicles are more efficient, have more range, and offer more convenience. Electric vehicles require endless hours of recharging and have less range, resulting in less efficient mobility. As the recent increase in the promotion of 15-minute cities demonstrates, mobility is something that globalists wish to limit or eradicate along with individual liberties. Traditional forms of energy enable these things, hence the globalist desire to destroy or significantly impair them by the year 2030.

A 15-minute city is one in which all necessities (as determined by government) are located within walking distance and there is no need to travel. These are the prison cities mentioned in the prescient documentary film *Endgame* which was years ahead of its time. It seems this method of city planning is being referenced on page 21: "By 2030, enhance inclusive and sustainable urbanization and capacity for participatory, integrated and sustainable human settlement planning and management in all countries" along with "expanding public transport" which is necessary for when they finally eradicate all private ownership of vehicles.

On page 21, they state their goal to "reduce inequalities of outcome". Almost anyone would agree with the ideal of decreasing inequality of opportunity. It is a hallmark of freedom that everyone should have the same opportunity to achieve success in life. But equality of outcome comes with a litany of consequences. This would mean that Lazy Jack who stays home playing video games and getting high receives the same compensation as Blue Collar Bob who works 14 hour days to earn his keep. Why would Bob continue to contribute to society when choosing unemployment yields the same outcome? Motivation is dead in such a system, and that is what they want: a universal basic income. Nobody gets ahead.

As stated in Klaus Schwab's Great Reset book, companies will be coerced into adopting globalist policies. This is what is meant in Agenda 2030 by the statement on page 22: "Encourage companies, especially large and transnational companies, to adopt sustainable practices and to integrate sustainability information into their reporting cycle." Companies who refuse to participate will be penalized.

More Druidic Mother-Earth worshipping Georgia Guidestone drivel is regurgitated on page 23 as lifestyles are encouraged that are "in harmony with nature" and we see a call to "integrate climate change measures into national policies."

On page 34: "Meeting every four years under the auspices of the General Assembly, the HLPF will provide high-level political guidance on the Agenda and its implementation, identify progress and emerging challenges and mobilize further actions to accelerate implementation. The next HLPF, under the auspices of the General Assembly, will take place in 2019, with the cycle of meetings thus reset, in order to maximize coherence with the Quadrennial Comprehensive Policy Review process." Agenda 2030 was introduced in 2015. The next HLPF (high level political forum) was four years later in 2019, just preceding the COVID-19 pandemic. The next meeting is scheduled for July 10-19, 2023. Hopefully there is no surprise awaiting us the following year as there was the year after the 2019 HLPF.

To further expound on what the 2030 Agenda might bring, I reference a WEF affiliate article from prepareforchange.net entitled, *8 Predications for the World in 2030*. Some of these projections may sound familiar.

1)   All products will have become services (own nothing).

2)   There is a global price on carbon.

3)   US dominance is over. We have a handful of global powers.

4)   Farewell hospital, hello home-spital (robotic tubes and bio-printed organs instead of scalpels).

5)   We are eating much less meat.

6)   Today's Syrian refugees, tomorrow's CEO's (making the case for open migration).

7)   The values that built the West will have been tested to the breaking point

8)   By the 2030's we'll be ready to move humans toward the red planet.

Kopf

Scenarios for the Future of Technology and International Development

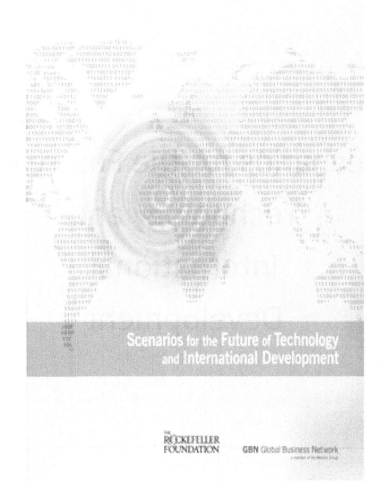

Scenarios for the Future of Technology and International Development

THE ROCKEFELLER FOUNDATION   GBN Global Business Network

This document from The Rockefeller Foundation was published in May of 2010. After extensive research, four future scenarios were developed to examine how government can use technology to shape the future within the context of emergent crises, one of which includes a viral pandemic which is why you may have heard lately about Operation Lockstep, though it is not an operation (or is it?) but rather the pandemic scenario contained in this report. There is a focus on vaccines in Lock Step as well as in the other non-pandemic scenarios.

The document begins with a letter from Judith Rodin, the President of the Rockefeller Foundation, who explains that "scenario planning has great potential for use in philanthropy to identify unique interventions, simulate and rehearse important decisions that could have profound implications, and highlight previously undiscovered areas of connection and intersection." She also notes that this is about exploring the "future of globalization."

The introduction explains why scenario-planning must take place (because the future is unpredictable) almost as though they are a guilty party providing an alibi, knowing how it will look when the things they are discussing come to pass. We are assured on page 9 that "Importantly, scenarios are not predictions."

The authors explain, "this project did not set out to identify a set of exact, yet-to-be-invented technologies that will help shape and change the future. Rather, the goal was to gain a broader and richer understanding of different paths along which technology could develop."

A common argument I hear when presenting strangely prescient government or NGO exercises such as this is that these exercises are just the normal part of our loving, caring governments taking preparatory action by planning for harmful contingencies and that these are not unusual but take place all the time. It is true that hypothetical scenario exercises such as war games have been taking place for years, but untrue that they have always taken place in the unlikely concentration that we see suddenly appear in 2019, which we will look more closely at later. In fact, their own game theory documentation acknowledges this.

In Scenarios for the Future of Technology and International Development, which I will now refer to as SFTID to save ink, there are two "critical uncertainties" identified that form the basis of the four scenarios presented. These are 1) how strong or weak political and economic alignment is, and 2) how high or low adaptive capacity is. The political and economic alignment axis is a measure of how cohesive the global control structure is, and the adaptive capacity axis is a measure of how receptive people will be to newly imposed regulations. Thus, the scenarios:

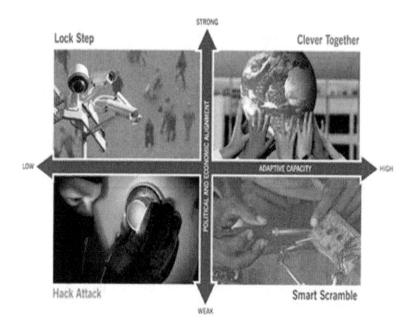

Page 17 explains, "Each scenario tells a story of how the world, and in particular the developing world, might progress over the next 15 to 20 years, with an emphasis on those elements relating to the use of different technologies and the interaction of these technologies with the lives of the poor and vulnerable... Please keep in mind that the scenarios in this report are stories, not forecasts..."

The first scenario discussed is **Lock Step:** "A world of tighter top-down government control and more authoritarian leadership, with limited innovation and growing citizen pushback."

Page 12 begins describing the scenario: "In 2012, the pandemic that the world had been anticipating for years finally hit. Unlike 2009's H1N1, this new influenza strain — originating from wild geese — was extremely virulent and deadly. Even the most pandemic-prepared nations were quickly overwhelmed when the virus streaked around the world, infecting nearly 20 percent of the global population and killing 8 million in just seven months, the majority of them healthy young adults. The pandemic also had a deadly effect on economies: international mobility of both people and goods screeched to a halt, debilitating industries like tourism and breaking global supply chains. Even locally, normally bustling shops and office buildings sat empty for months, devoid of both employees and customers. The pandemic blanketed the planet— though disproportionate numbers died in Africa, Southeast Asia, and Central America, where the virus spread like wildfire in the absence of official containment protocols. But even in developed countries, containment was a challenge. The United States' initial policy of "strongly discouraging" citizens from flying proved deadly in its leniency, accelerating the spread of the virus not just within the U.S. but across borders. However, a few countries did fare better — China in particular. The Chinese government's quick imposition and enforcement of mandatory quarantine for all citizens, as well as its instant and near-hermetic sealing off of all borders, saved millions of lives, stopping the spread of the virus far earlier than in other countries and enabling a swifter post-pandemic recovery."

"China's government was not the only one that took extreme measures to protect its citizens from risk and exposure. During the pandemic, national leaders around the world flexed their authority and imposed airtight rules and restrictions, from the mandatory wearing of facemasks to body-temperature checks at the entries to communal spaces like train stations and supermarkets. Even after the pandemic faded, this more authoritarian control and oversight of citizens and their activities stuck and even intensified. In order to protect themselves from the spread of increasingly global problems — from pandemics and transnational terrorism to environmental crises and rising poverty — leaders around the world took a firmer grip on power. At first, the notion of a more controlled world gained wide acceptance and approval. Citizens willingly gave up some of their sovereignty — and their privacy — to more paternalistic states in exchange for greater safety and stability. Citizens were more tolerant, and even eager, for top-down direction and oversight, and national leaders had more latitude to impose order in the ways they saw fit. In developed countries, this heightened oversight took many forms: biometric IDs for all citizens, for example, and tighter regulation of key industries whose stability was deemed vital to national interests. In many developed countries, enforced cooperation with a suite of new regulations and agreements slowly but steadily restored both order and, importantly, economic growth. Across the developing world, however, the story was different — and much more variable. Top-down authority took different forms in different countries, hinging largely on the capacity, caliber, and intentions of their leaders. In countries with strong and thoughtful leaders, citizens' overall economic status and quality of life increased. In India, for example, air quality drastically improved after 2016, when the government outlawed high-emitting vehicles. In Ghana, the introduction of ambitious government programs to improve basic infrastructure and ensure the availability of clean water for all her people led to a sharp decline in water-borne diseases. But more authoritarian leadership worked less well — and in some cases tragically — in countries run by irresponsible elites who used their increased power to pursue their own interests at the expense of their citizens."

"There were other downsides, as the rise of virulent nationalism created new hazards... By 2025, people seemed to be growing weary of so much top-down control... The feeling lingered that sooner or later, something would inevitably upset the neat order that the world's governments had worked so hard to establish."

Each scenario is followed by a section that was included "to offer a sense of the contest for technological innovation, taking into consideration the pace, geography, and key creators." The technology trends and applications we might see according to the authors include:

- Scanners using advanced functional magnetic resonance imaging technology become the norm at airports and other public areas to detect abnormal behavior that may indicate antisocial intent.

- New diagnostics are developed to detect communicable diseases. The application of health screening also changes; screening becomes a prerequisite for release from a hospital or prison.

- Driven by protectionism and national security concerns, nations create their own independent, regionally defined IT networks, mimicking China's firewalls. Governments have varying degrees of success in policing internet traffic.

The next scenario is **Clever Together**: "A world in which highly coordinated and successful strategies emerge for addressing both urgent and entrenched worldwide issues."

This is what could be called the climate change scenario and it begins on page 26. It is characterized by increased surveillance and vaccination. The eradication of meat also finds its way into this scenario in which "carbon dioxide levels were climbing precipitously, creating new urgency and pressure for governments (really everyone) to do something fast."

"Centralized global oversight and governance structures sprang up, not just for energy use but also for disease and technology standards. Such systems and structures required far greater levels of transparency, which in turn required more tech-enabled data collection, processing, and feedback. Enormous, benign "sousveillance" systems allowed citizens to access data — all publicly available — in real time and react. Nation-states lost some of their power and importance as global architecture strengthened and regional governance structures emerged. International oversight entities like the UN took on new levels of authority."

"New inexpensive technologies like better medical diagnostics and more effective vaccines improved healthcare delivery and health outcomes. Companies, NGOs, and governments — often acting together — launched pilot programs and learning labs to figure out how to best meet the needs of particular communities, increasing the knowledge base of what worked and what didn't. Pharmaceuticals giants released thousands of drug compounds shown to be effective against diseases like malaria into the public domain as part of an "open innovation" agenda; they also opened their archives of R&D on neglected diseases deemed not commercially viable, offering seed funding to scientists who wanted to carry the research forward."

Among the technology trends listed in the "technology" section for Clever Together are:

- The cost of capturing data through nano sensors and smart networks falls precipitously. In many developing countries, this leads to a proliferation of new and useful services, including "sousveillance" mechanisms that improve governance and enable more efficient use of government resources.

- Intelligent electricity, water distribution, and transportation systems develop in urban areas. In these "smart cities," internet access is seen as a basic right by the late 2010s.

- A malaria vaccine is developed and deployed broadly – saving millions of lives in the developing world.

- Advances in low-cost mind-controlled prosthetics aid the 80 percent of global amputees who live in developing countries.

- Flexible and rapid mobile payment systems drive dynamic economic growth in the developing world, while the developed world is hampered by entrenched banking interests and regulation.

Each technology section is followed by a story that offers a glimpse into what life could look like in the offered scenario. In the Clever Together scenario, we meet Alec whose "research team had been working for months to fabricate a new meat product." What this has to do with anything else in the scenario, I know not, but I mention it here only to highlight the strange obsession that the globalists have with creating synthetic meat.

The next scenario is **Hack Attack**: "An economically unstable and shock-prone world in which governments weaken, criminals thrive, and dangerous innovations emerge." This could be called the natural disaster scenario and it is characterized by increased crime rates, cyber threats, and vaccines that are tainted because the government didn't have control over them. There are also plugs for how good GMO's are and how bad patriotism and the traditional family are.

Once again, vaccines find their way into this scenario. On page 35 we read, "Criminal networks also grew highly skilled at counterfeiting licit goods through reverse engineering. Many of these "rip-offs" and copycats were of poor quality or downright dangerous. In the context of weak health systems, corruption, and inattention to standards — either within countries or from global bodies like the World Health Organization — tainted vaccines entered the public health systems of several African countries. In 2021, 600 children in Cote d'Ivoire died from a bogus Hepatitis B vaccine, which paled in comparison to the scandal sparked by mass deaths from a tainted anti-malarial drug years later. The deaths and resulting scandals sharply affected public confidence in vaccine delivery; parents not just in Africa but elsewhere began to avoid vaccinating their children, and it wasn't long before infant and child mortality rates rose to levels not seen since the 1970s. Technology hackers were also hard at work. Internet scams and pyramid schemes plagued inboxes. Meanwhile, more sophisticated hackers attempted to take down corporations, government systems, and banks via phishing scams and database information heists, and their many successes generated billions of dollars in losses. Desperate to protect themselves and their intellectual property, the few multinationals still thriving enacted strong, increasingly complex defensive measures. Patent applications skyrocketed and patent thickets proliferated, as companies fought to claim and control even the tiniest innovations. Security measures and screenings tightened. This "wild west" environment had a profound impact on innovation. The threat of being hacked and the presence of so many thefts and fakes lowered the incentives to create "me first" rather than "me too" technologies. And so many patent thickets made the cross-pollination of ideas and research difficult at best. Blockbuster pharmaceuticals quickly became artifacts of the past, replaced by increased production of generics. Breakthrough innovations still happened in various industries, but they were focused more on technologies that could not be easily replicated or re-engineered. And once created, they were vigorously guarded by their inventors — or even by their nations. In 2022, a biofuel breakthrough in Brazil was protected as a national treasure and used as a bargaining chip in trade with other countries."

The scenario goes on to describe issues that people began to have due to malicious hackers, though "not all of the "hacking" was bad. Genetically modified crops (GMOs) and do-it- yourself (DIY) biotech became backyard and garage activities, producing important advances... Those who couldn't buy their way out of chaos — which was most people — retreated to whatever "safety" they could find. With opportunity frozen and global mobility at anear standstill — no place wanted more people, especially more poor people — it was often a retreat to the familiar: family ties, religious beliefs, or even national allegiance."

The reader may notice a disdain for family, faith, and patriotism in these NWO documents. Nationalism is the antithesis to Globalism, hence phrases like "virulent nationalism" as stated in the Lockstep scenario.

Among the technology trends listed in the "technology" section for Hack Attack are:

- Echoing the rise of synthetic chemicals in the nineteenth century, synthetic biology, often state-funded, is used to "grow" resources and foodstuffs that have become scarce.

- New threats like weaponized biological pathogens and destructive botnets dominate public attention, but enduring technologies, like the AK-47, also remain weapons of choice for global guerrillas.

- The internet is overrun with spam and security threats and becomes strongly associated with illicit activity — especially on "dark webs" where no government can monitor, identify, or restrict activities.

The story that Hack Attack concludes with can be mostly dismissed, though it is interesting that in it, "counterfeit vaccines were being manufactured. But so were GMO seeds. And synthetic proteins." One would expect a greater diversity of technologies than vaccines and synthetic proteins in a variety of hypothetical scenarios (that are not to be regarded as predictions) such as these, but the same ideas continue to reemerge.

The final scenario in SFTID is called **Smart Scramble**: "An economically depressed world in which individuals and communities develop localized, makeshift solutions to a growing set of problems." This might be called the global recession scenario. And yes, vaccines are somehow a part of this one too as an MIT professor and resettled pharma researcher "invent a cheap, edible vaccine against tuberculosis that dramatically reduced childhood mortality (p. 44)."

The message of Smart Scramble is that all technological development should be managed by the government. "Local experiments and innovations could neither scale nor boost overall growth... without major progress in global economic integration and collaboration, many worried that good ideas would stay isolated (p. 45)."

Among the technology trends listed in the "technology" section for Smart Scramble are:

• Energy technology improvements are geared more toward efficiency—getting more from existing sources of power— than new-generation technologies, though some local improvements in generating and distributing wind and geothermal energy do occur.

• Breakdowns in the global medicine supply chain accelerate the emergence of locally bioengineered super-strength homeopathic remedies, which replace antibiotics in the dispensaries of many developing-world hospitals.

• Widespread micro-manufacturing, using 3D printers, enables the fabrication of replacement components for engines and machines, allowing "perpetual maintenance" to compensate for broken trade links.

• Garden allotments proliferate in mega-cities as new urban-dwellers seek to supplement a scarce food supply and maintain their agricultural heritage.

The document draws the following conclusion on page 49: "Technologies will affect governance, and governance in turn will play a major role in determining what technologies are developed and who those technologies are intended, and able, to benefit."

We know who they are intended to benefit. They are intended to benefit the self-proclaimed elite. As far as I'm concerned, they can have it. These technologies lead inevitably toward transhumanism, which will be explored in greater detail in the following pages.

Kopf

The SPARS Pandemic

THE

SPARS PANDEMIC

2025 - 2028

A Futuristic Scenario for Public Health Risk Communicators

THE JOHNS HOPKINS CENTER FOR HEALTH SECURITY

The Johns Hopkins Center for Health Security is one of the globalist resources for research that can be weaponized against free people. In October of 2017 they published the SPARS pandemic scenario which involves a novel coronavirus originating in Southeast Asia and quickly reaching pandemic status. Set from the year 2025 to 2028, this apparently hypothetical scenario is an exercise in how to ensure that the people are receiving only government approved narratives about safety protocol and more specifically, how to keep people invested in receiving vaccinations after it becomes abundantly clear that they are causing harm.

The first page offers their rationale for the exercise: "The following narrative comprises a futuristic scenario that illustrates communication dilemmas concerning medical countermeasures (MCMs) that could plausibly emerge in the not-so-distant future."

You don't say. Not-so-distant is right, especially in light of the glaring similarities between this document and real-world events that later took place. The authors assure us that this exercise is intended for the protection of the public, and we are assured by skeptics that exercises such as these have always taken place. In a way they have. Back in 2001, Dark Winter, a smallpox scenario, was completed. The next exercise completed by the same organizers did not occur until the Atlantic Storm scenario in 2005. These were both simulations involving the release of bioweapons by terrorists. Years later, the scenarios morphed from intentionally released bioweapons to naturally occurring pandemics as described in the Clade-X exercise (2018), Event 201 (2019), and most recently, Catastrophic Contagion (2022). There are several more that suddenly appear in 2019 that we will review later.

To the best of my research, we in the United States had a total of 3 or 4 high-level pandemic exercises conducted in all our history up until 2017 (fewer if you eliminate the bioweapon drills). Then suddenly, just before COVID-19 hit, we had a minimum of 6 emerge all at once, most of those being published in October of 2019, just two months before the real event. We'll get to those later.

The preface of SPARS begins, "Ultimately, a world comprised of isolated and highly fragmented communities with widespread access to information technology—dubbed "the echo-chamber"— was selected as the future in which the prospective scenario would take place."

This is a scenario that would assist them in learning how to best control a locked-down society that still had internet access for information. Also in the preface is the disclaimer that "this prospective scenario is not intended to predict events to come." However, you will see that many of the hypothetical situations did in fact come to pass as though forecasted. In fact, just two paragraphs down from the disclaimer, the scenario environment is laid out which introduces the President, Randall Archer, as having previously served as Vice President, as is the case with Joe Biden, a minor synchronicity in comparison to some of the later events described.

On page 3 there is an explanation for the purpose of the scenario: "This scenario was designed to illustrate the public health risk communication challenges associated with distribution of emergency medical countermeasures during an infectious disease pandemic." Translation: How to convince the public to get vaccinated.

SPARS is an acronym for St. Paul Acute Respiratory Syndrome as the first cases in the United States were among residents of St. Paul. They tested negative for influenza and it was later determined that they were infected with a novel coronavirus originating from Southeast Asia. The virus erupted during flu season: "Given that flu season was just getting underway and that a rapid diagnostic test for SPARS-CoV infection was not yet available, CDC officials could not be sure if these were, in fact, true cases of SPARS (p. 5)."

As in the real world, the timing was ideal to conflate coronavirus infections with flu infections. You may recall that cases of influenza miraculously vanished during the great COVID-19 pandemic.

Further on page 5: "As transmission of SPARS was determined to occur via droplet spread, the CDC initially recommended that everyone diligently maintain hand hygiene and frequently disinfect potentially contaminated surfaces. CDC officials further urged anyone with severe flu-like symptoms to seek immediate medical attention. Public health officials were concerned that the upcoming Thanksgiving holiday and Black Friday shopping activities would facilitate the spread of SPARS."

Some researchers have noted that the CDC tweets offered on SPARS were nearly identical to the CDC's tweets regarding COVID-19.

CDC ✔
@CDCgov

Holiday travel plans? #StopSPARS by washing your hands and avoiding public places if you feel sick.

1:13 PM - 13 Nov 2025

460 Retweets 1,380 Likes

♡ 466   ↻ 460   ♡ 1K

CDC ✔
@CDCgov

If you feel ill: seek medical attention, use the #VampireCough and avoid others to prevent the spread of #SPARS. #StopSPARSSaturday

4:18 PM - 16 Nov 2025

893 Retweets 2,571 Likes

♡ 914   ↻ 893   ♡ 3K

CDC ✔
@CDCgov

Practice good #hygiene during your #Thanksgiving travels. Bring home leftovers, not #SPARS!

2:28 PM - 23 Nov 2025

802 Retweets 2,357 Likes

♡ 966   ↻ 802   ♡ 2K

CDC ✔
@CDCgov

#HappyThanksgiving! Be safe on #BlackFriday! If you brave the crowds, wash your hands often. If you feel sick, shop on #CyberMonday instead.

"At the outset of the SPARS outbreak, physicians' understanding of the disease stemmed primarily from extremely severe cases resulting in pneumonia or hypoxia that required hospitalization and extensive medical treatment. Mild cases of the disease, which produced symptoms including cough, fever, headaches, and malaise, were often perceived as the flu by the people who had them and consequently often went untreated and undiagnosed by medical personnel. As a result, early case fatality estimates were inflated (p. 6)."

Our own compromised media now reluctantly acknowledge that COVID-19 cases were indeed inflated. One can't have an effective pandemic without the big scary numbers to substantiate it, whether those numbers be fake or real.

One of the things that contributed a good deal to the fear of COVID-19 is what we were told about the incubation period, as was the case with SPARS: "First, the virus had an extended incubation period (seven to ten days) compared to its latent period (four to five days). Thus, infected persons could spread the virus for up to nearly a week before showing symptoms of the disease themselves (p. 6)."

On page 8, the reader is introduced to an unsafe MCM (medical countermeasure): "Based on previous trials in other coronavirus patients, the antiviral Kalocivir is the leading candidate; however, neither the efficacy nor safety profile has been determined for SPARS cases."

Page 9: "Kalocivir had shown some evidence of efficacy against other coronaviruses, and a small inventory of the drug was already a part of the Strategic National Stockpile (SNS) in anticipation of FDA approval, despite some concerns about potential adverse side effects."

That was precisely the case with COVID-19. The concern for potential adverse side-effects was hidden from the public, but a number of coronavirus vaccine studies advised exercising caution in moving forward with such vaccines in humans based on the immunopathology, death, and other side effects that occurred in the animal test subjects, or they determined that the vaccines should not be used at all.

This is further addressed in the fictionalized research paper on page 11: "Given the millions of vaccinations required for Region 7, this resulted in measurable losses to the animal population; however, these were acceptable compared to those from the respiratory infection itself."

Page 12: "Data provided by GMI suggested that the vaccine was effective at preventing SPARS-like illnesses in cows, pigs, and other hooved mammals, but internal trials revealed several worrisome side effects, including swollen legs, severe joint pain, and encephalitis leading to seizures or death."

Vaccine demonstrably unsafe and ineffective despite our claims to the contrary? No problem, we'll offer liability protection to the vaccine providers: "HHS Secretary Nagel agreed in principle to invoke the Public Readiness and Emergency Preparedness Act (PREP Act), thereby providing liability protection for CynBio and future vaccine providers in the event that vaccine recipients experienced any adverse effects (p. 12)."

Sound familiar?

Each chapter of SPARS concludes with a "communication dilemma" that consists of a few discussion questions. One of the questions posed in the communication dilemma of chapter 2 on page 10 is: "What kinds of outreach could public health agencies perform in advance of a crisis to mitigate any perceived lack of transparency?"

Are you beginning to see a theme emerge in these globalist documents? There is a focus on ensuring the appearance of righteousness. They are constantly trying to think of ways to not appear suspicious.

The communication dilemma following chapter 3 is also about "maintaining trust in government processes". The questions asked include:

- "How might federal health authorities avoid people possibly seeing an expedited SPARS vaccine development and testing process as somehow "rushed" and inherently flawed?"

- "How might federal health authorities respond to critics who propose that liability protection for SPARS vaccine manufacturers jeopardizes individual freedom and wellbeing?"

In 2017 they already knew what they would be doing, so they created the SPARS document as an exercise to brainstorm ways to get ahead of the narrative. If that isn't obvious yet, it will be.

"While initial hopes had been that Kalocivir would, in addition to treating the disease, prevent or reduce transmission, this was not the case (p.14)."

Over and over, we see the SPARS events come to life in real time as in the above headline, "SPARS Drug May be Ineffective. Use it Anyway". That is what we are now being told about all of the COVID-19 vaccines, whether Johnson and Johnson, Astra Zeneca, Moderna, or Pfizer.

Chapter 4 is about how to appropriately tailor public health messages to particular demographics. They use the Navajo as an example on page 17, stating how the Navajo Area Indian Health Services director made the mistake of using a fear-based message to get Navajos vaccinated: "While the intent of the director was to increase the number of Navajo seeking treatment for SPARS, the modified message, which was widely distributed throughout tribal areas, backfired. Fewer Navajo came forward in the following weeks for treatment from the NAIHS for SPARS-like symptoms. Sensing a mistake had been made, the director reached out to tribal leadership. After intensive dialog the messaging of the NAIHS was changed to reflect Navajo beliefs in sustaining life and eschewing a focus on death. Specifically, the fear-based messaging was replaced with positive messages including, "Seeing health care providers for SPARS-like symptoms can help you and your family members live long and happy lives."

What an important lesson in propaganda and social manipulation. To further explore social control methodologies, the question is asked on page 18: "How could social media have been used to supplement traditional methods of collecting data about Kalocivir's effectiveness and side effects?"

This leads us to Chapter 5 which addresses the very important issue of how to control the narrative in an age when people are able to freely share information on social media. It seems as though they were well aware that there would be videos of fainting nurses and many people suffering from various side effects such as seizures and facial paralysis erupting all over social media, so they endeavored to get ahead of all that in this document. The example they provide is on page 19: "Despite the negative response, public health agencies continued to make progress until February, when a video of a three-year-old boy in North Carolina — who was hospitalized with SPARS and began projectile vomiting immediately after taking a dose of Kalocivir — went viral. In the video clip, the boy's physician administers a pediatric dose of liquid Kalocivir; a few moments later, the boy begins vomiting profusely, chokes, and then faints while his mother shrieks in the background."

Their fictional (now realized) response to this is, "FDA and other government agencies quickly attempted to remind the public that correlation does not equate to causation, and that vomiting was not a known side effect of Kalocivir (p.20)."

"Correlation does not equal causation" is the perfect alibi, for it is nearly unfalsifiable. Even using an extreme example, such as someone dying in a plane crash, causation can be denied. The idiot skeptic may say, "Well we don't KNOW the plane crash killed him, he could have died of a brain aneurysm or something."

The communication dilemma of chapter 5 is, "Responding to the Power of Graphic Images…".

The question is posed, "What MCM communication challenges and opportunities are likely to emerge among up-and-coming youth audiences who are avid consumers of interactive and visual forms of information?"

In other words, people are going to see the adverse side-effects of our "vaccines", especially younger people. How can we brainwash them into not believing what is before their very eyes?

Chapter 7, beginning on page 25, identifies public disinterest as an issue. "By May 2026, public interest in SPARS had begun to wane... the new, lower case fatality rate estimate led the public to grow increasingly hostile toward continued SPARS messaging... In order to overcome the public's disinterest, the CDC and FDA, in concert with other government agencies and their social media experts, began developing a new pubic health messaging campaign... agency officials enlisted the help of well-known scientists, celebrities, and government officials to make short videos... President Jaclyn Bennett, BZee, a popular hip-hop star, and Paul Farmer, co-founder of Partners in Health and renowned global health expert."

Let's break that down. Public interest in COVID-19 will start to wane. That is not good because we need to keep the crisis alive in order to meet our sustainability development goals (New World Order). We need to recruit well-known public figures to augment our propaganda in public video messages. Let's bring in President Jaclyn Bennett (former Presidents Clinton, Bush, and Obama did collaborate on a such a video), BZee (have you seen Run DMC's cringey "get the vaccine" video?), and Paul Farmer (Anthony Fauci).

Page 29 mentions a satirical news feed that was problematic to the aims of the government's and NGO's public messaging. One has to wonder if they may have been anticipating trouble from the Babylon Bee. Whether they were or not, they were definitely anticipating trouble from social media as they identified "incorrect messages" being shared on public forums. The communication dilemma questions posed on page 39 include:

- Why is active monitoring of the "information sea" in which the public is swimming critical to the efforts of authorities to create conditions and provide information that support recommended public health behaviors?

- How might a strong social media presence allow the federal government to anticipate potential communication issues before they become full-fledged crises?

Further reflecting the reality of the initial COVID-19 scare in the SPARS document is the inclusion of a massive power outage event which did in fact occur in Texas during an unusual cold spell. People died. Though in SPARS, the power failure and subsequent rolling blackouts occurred in Washington, Idaho, Montana, and British Columbia: "...the power grid at the Grand Coulee Dam in eastern Washington State experienced a catastrophic failure (p.40)."

This has little to do with a pandemic other than the loss of power inhibiting public messaging to promote vaccines, though I thought it worth noting that some of the non-pandemic events that occurred in real life also showed up in the SPARS document, such as the power outage and Black Lives Matter making an appearance (though in SPARS it was unrelated to George Floyd of course – p.46).

Also just as in real life, Japan rejects the American vaccines in the SPARS document. On page 49, a news article reads, "Prime Minister Kideyoshi Miyazaki created a stir today after announcing that the Pharmaceuticals and Medical Devices Agency would not approve Corovax for the prevention of St. Paul Acute Respiratory Syndrome cases in Japan. Citing Corovax's side effects and recent advances made by scientists at the University of Tokyo's Institute of Medical Science, Miyazaki said that Japan expected to roll out its own SPARS vaccine in early 2027."

Luckily, they prepared for this in their communication dilemma on page 51: "In an increasingly interconnected global communication environment, how could US health officials be better poised to explain the rationale for their continued recommendation of the US-based Corovax vaccine when Japan regulators opt not to approve the vaccine?"

How indeed? How do governments and health agencies continue to promote something that has been rejected by numerous other countries due to the associated risks (a better question to ponder is *why* would they)? Unfortunately, the real answer may be that people are so insanely stupid that they will drink rat poison as long as their government tells them to.

Back in 2017 they were already hard at work exploring fact-checking methods. "The US government added a new, aggressive advertising campaign to its pro-vaccination efforts. This campaign provided targeted internet advertisements to individuals as they conducted web searches or visited anti-vaccination websites. If someone searched Google for "Corovax side effects," for example, a sidebar advertisement appeared on the results page explaining the benefits of the vaccine. Likewise, if someone wished to view the Kalocivir vomiting video on YouTube, they would first have to watch either a montage of pictures illustrating the effects of SPARS or a clip of Paul Farmer's explanation of Corovax's benefits. This advertisement campaign required government officials to leverage relationships in the information technology industry (p.55)."

Chapter 17 is entitled, "Vaccine Injury". It begins on page 59: "As time passed and more people across the United

States were vaccinated, claims of adverse side effects began to emerge. Several parents claimed that their children were experiencing neurological symptoms similar to those seen among livestock exposed to the GMI vaccine."

Page 60: "Nearing the end of 2027, reports of new neurological symptoms began to emerge. After showing no adverse side effects for nearly a year, several vaccine recipients slowly began to experience symptoms such as blurry vision, headaches, and numbness in their extremities."

I know people in my personal life who began to experience these very symptoms following vaccination. Eric Clapton (not in my personal life) has a lot to say about numbness in his extremities caused by the vaccine that nearly ended his career. Note however, that in the SPARS document these symptoms do not emerge until long after the vaccine is administered. Furthermore, they acknowledge that the more long-term side effects cannot yet be known. Also note that means that it cannot be claimed that the vaccines are safe, whether for SPARS or COVID.

The question of how to respond to the public when it becomes undeniable that the vaccine is causing injuries is posed on page 62: "How might advance development and testing of recovery messages that specifically address the topics of adverse side effects and the NVICTF help improve health authorities' ability to respond to public distress about medical issues emerging after a MCM campaign? What are some messages that would warrant such testing?"

Chapter 18, "Acknowledging Loss", answers the question of how to respond to the American people when it becomes irrefutably apparent that the vaccines are killing people. The answer is to simply say thanks for complying: "The primary message would be one of gratitude to the American people for remaining strong during the pandemic. Another key message would convey appreciation for adhering to public health recommendations, including vaccination, to hasten the end of the pandemic in the face of considerable uncertainty."

The final chapter warns that "the virus persists in domesticated animal reservoirs". Funny way of saying "farms", which are currently being attacked by globalist policies as the New World Order seeks the demolition of agriculture as foretold by Lord Birkenhead 100 years ago. To expand on that, "they anticipate that future outbreaks will continue to emerge unless countries maintain widespread vaccination coverage (p. 66)."

And finally, in their conclusion, they include a statement that functions as an admonishment that any claims of the virus coming from a biolab is just a wild conspiracy theory: "Conspiracy theories also proliferated across social media, suggesting that the virus had been purposely created and introduced to the population by drug companies or that it had escaped from a government lab secretly testing bioweapons (p.66)."

You know, like the Wuhan lab just down the street from the wet market that led to the shutdown of the entire world because of a bowl of bat soup, which, according to organizations like the Johns Hopkins Center for Health Security, is NOT a crazy conspiracy theory, but a virus escaping or being released from a lab that deals with viruses is.

More from Johns Hopkins to come.

Dark Winter, Atlantic Storm, Clade-X, Event 201, and Catastrophic Contagion

FINAL SCRIPT – DARK WINTER EXERCISE

DARK WINTER

Bioterrorism Exercise
Andrews Air Force Base
June 22-23, 2001

Dark Winter is a tabletop exercise completed by the Johns Hopkins Center for Civilian Biodefense in 2001 concerning a terrorist release of smallpox. Though it is ostensibly about smallpox as a bioweapon, the authors are sure to mention that the drill is for any virus. The document seems to advocate for using the smallpox attack as an excuse to initiate nuclear war, roll out vaccinations quickly, and only promote vaccines from the United States while prohibiting others. Also included are matters of racial tension, forced quarantine, and border concerns. Some quotes include: "Americans can no longer take basic civil liberties such as freedom of assembly or travel for granted" and "Smallpox shatters image of US as superpower", which is, of course, exactly the result hoped for by globalist actors.

I do not believe that this exercise is obsolete despite it having aged for two decades. Rather I tend to think Dark Winter was very influential to the bad actors currently destroying our government from within as it is a phrase still on their lips (both Joe Biden and Anthony Fauci have referenced a "dark winter" ahead).

The disease containment recommendations on pages 34 and 35 include:

- Encourage voluntary home isolation of contacts using NG and DOD assets to supply food/track fevers, etc. (mandatory grouping of infected and non-infected contacts too dangerous)

- Penalties for promulgating dangerous information

- Establish federal travel restrictions

- Economic impacts

- Cancel all public gatherings in affected stated, non-essential meetings of >50 people elsewhere

The vaccine doses are limited in availability and may be fatal to about 1 in every 5,000 people who receive it (p.19). One of the decision points mentioned on this page is whether vaccines should be voluntary or mandatory.

On page 27 it is noted that federal troops may be used for law enforcement if the President invokes the Insurrection Act to quell civil disturbances. On page 28, justification for declaring martial law under 32 C.F.R. 501.4 is presented.

The disease containment options listed on page 34 include:

- Restrict smallpox patients to dedicated facilities? – voluntary vs. mandatory

- Assemble contacts of patients in designated sites? – voluntary vs. mandatory

- Establish national travel policies? – voluntary vs. mandatory

- Legislation to prohibit dangerous information?

The presentation of Dark Winter is more chaotic than that of SPARS and many other tabletop exercises and it has recently become a little harder to locate as it appears that the Johns Hopkins Center for Health Security has removed the report from their website, however, they do include a listing of the 5 pandemic exercises they have completed over the years, the majority of them most recently:

"The Center hosts a series of tabletop exercises to illustrate the high-level strategic decisions and policies stakeholders will need to pursue to diminish the consequences of a severe pandemic. The training tabletop exercises are based on fictional scenarios and inputs. These exercises are teaching and training resources for public health and government officials."

Catastrophic Contagion

The Johns Hopkins Center for Health Security, in partnership with WHO and the Bill & Melinda Gates Foundation, conducted *Catastrophic Contagion*, a pandemic tabletop exercise at the Grand Challenges Annual Meeting in Brussels, Belgium.
October 23, 2022

Event 201

The Johns Hopkins Center for Health Security in partnership with the World Economic Forum and the Bill and Melinda Gates Foundation hosted *Event 201*, a high-level pandemic exercise on October 18, 2019, in New York, NY. The purpose of the exercise was to illustrate the pandemic preparedness efforts, response decisions, and cooperation required from global businesses, governments, and public health leaders that the world will need to diminish the large-scale economic and societal consequences of a severe pandemic.
October 18, 2019

Clade X

The Center hosted a pandemic tabletop exercise in Washington, D.C., in May 2018. The goal of this exercise ("Clade X") was to illustrate high-level strategic decisions and policies that the United States and the world will need to pursue in order to diminish the consequences of a severe pandemic. It addressed a pressing current concern, present plausible solutions, and be experientially engaging.
May 15, 2018

Atlantic Storm

Atlantic Storm was a ministerial table-top exercise convened by the Center for Biosecurity, the Center for Transatlantic Relations of the Johns Hopkins University, and the Transatlantic Biosecurity Network. The exercise used a

fictitious scenario designed to mimic a summit of transatlantic leaders forced to respond to a bioterrorist attack. The event website provides a comprehensive overview of the exercise and access to all materials and multimedia, including Atlantic Storm Interactive, and the after-action report, "Navigating the Storm."
January 14, 2005

Dark Winter

The *Dark Winter* exercise portrayed a fictional scenario depicting a covert smallpox attack on US citizens. The scenario is set in 3 successive NSC meetings that take place over 2 weeks. The exercise was held at Andrews Air Force Base, Washington, DC. The Dark Winter script and other event materials are available through the conference web pages.
June 22-23, 2001

With the advancement of technology, the documentation of these events appears to have become less dependent on physical printable paper reports in favor of video recordings of the live-streamed events made available online. Therefore, there is little more to be said of each individual pandemic exercise without risking redundancy. I led with Dark Winter as live-streaming was not such a popular medium at the time of its creation and there are no video presentations to reference for it online, though there is a brief, disjointed report to reference, as seen above.

Of the Hopkins reports, Event 201 is the most interesting to me if only due to the timing of it. It is one of many other reports from other organizers that emerged during exactly the same month and year, October 2019, which immediately preceded the COVID-19 pandemic.

From the website:

When/where

Friday, October 18, 2019
8:45 a.m. – 12:30 p.m.
The Pierre hotel
New York, NY

Audience

An invitation-only audience of nearly 130 people attended the exercises, and a livestream of the event was available to everyone.

About the Event 201 exercise

"Event 201 was a 3.5-hour pandemic tabletop exercise that simulated a series of dramatic, scenario-based facilitated discussions, confronting difficult, true-to-life dilemmas associated with response to a hypothetical, but scientifically plausible, pandemic. 15 global business, government, and public health leaders were players in the simulation exercise that highlighted unresolved real-world policy and economic issues that could be solved with sufficient political will, financial investment, and attention now and in the future."

"The exercise consisted of pre-recorded news broadcasts, live "staff" briefings, and moderated discussions on specific topics. These issues were carefully designed in a compelling narrative that educated the participants and the audience."

"The Johns Hopkins Center for Health Security, World Economic Forum, and Bill & Melinda Gates Foundation jointly propose these recommendations."

Among the recommendations, the Event 201 "Call to Action" states that "companies with operations focused on logistics, social media, or distribution systems will be needed to enable governments' emergency response, risk communications, and medical countermeasure distribution efforts during a pandemic."

"...this virtual stockpile model could be expanded to augment WHO's ability to distribute vaccines and therapeutics to countries in the greatest need during a severe pandemic. This should also include any available experimental vaccine stockpiles for any WHO R&D Blueprint pathogens to deploy in a clinical trial during outbreaks in collaboration with CEPI, GAVI, and WHO."

" Improved decision-making, coordination, and communications between the public and private sectors, relating to risk, travel advisories, import/export restrictions, and border measures will be needed."

Don't forget about the "liability protection in certain cases" as stated further down the page. And even farther down, "This will require addressing legal and regulatory barriers among other issues" ("new technologies and industrial approaches that will allow concomitant distributed manufacturing").

"A severe pandemic would greatly interfere with workforce health, business operations, and the movement of goods and services." ...which is just perfect for the Great Reset. Necessary in fact. It's the perfect problem for the greatest problem-reaction-solution ever perpetrated on mankind. There could be no better opportunity to build back better.

They warn that "Much of the economic harm resulting from a pandemic is likely to be due to counterproductive behavior of individuals, companies, and countries."

In other words, there will be people who do not comply with the Draconian measures that we will ensure are instituted. Miscreants, purveyors of misinformation, and people with detestable religious or patriotic leanings will need to be dealt with. Hence, the final recommendation:

"Governments and the private sector should assign a greater priority to developing methods to combat mis- and disinformation prior to the next pandemic response. Governments will need to partner with traditional and social media companies to research and develop nimble approaches to countering misinformation. This will require developing the ability to flood media with fast, accurate, and consistent information. Public health authorities should work with private employers and trusted community leaders such as faith leaders, to promulgate factual information to employees and citizens. Trusted, influential private-sector employers should create the capacity to readily and reliably augment public messaging, manage rumors and misinformation, and amplify credible information to support emergency public communications. National public health agencies should work in close collaboration with WHO to create the capability to rapidly develop and release consistent health messages. For their part, media companies should commit to ensuring that authoritative messages are prioritized and that false messages are suppressed including though the use of technology."

Preparedness for a High-Impact Respiratory Pathogen Pandemic

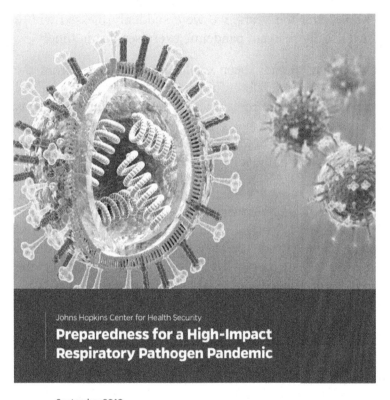

Johns Hopkins Center for Health Security

Preparedness for a High-Impact Respiratory Pathogen Pandemic

September 2019

JOHNS HOPKINS
BLOOMBERG SCHOOL
of PUBLIC HEALTH | Center for **Health Security**

In addition to Event 201, there have been 5 other pandemic studies and tabletop exercises completed in 2019, one of them in June, but most of them in September and October, just preceding COVID-19. How fortuitous that despite previous pandemic exercises having been completed only once in a great while over the years, we were suddenly blessed with 6 very specifically relevant pandemic exercises just in time!

Since we have already been exploring documents from the Johns Hopkins Center for Moloch Worship (as I like to call it), I am beginning the remainder of the pandemic documents with Hopkins' Preparedness for a High-Impact Respiratory Pathogen Pandemic from September, 2019, just before a high-impact respiratory pathogen pandemic struck.

The executive summary inadvertently does away with the argument I tend to hear when presenting these exercises as evidence that the COVID-19 pandemic was planned. I am told that pandemic exercises are very common and their existence in no way substantiates my claims. But apparently the exercises themselves disagree. According to Preparedness for a High-Impact Respiratory Pathogen Pandemic, which I will call HIRPP moving forward: "While there has been some focus on improving international and national capacities for pandemic influenza, specifically after the 2009 H1N1 pandemic, there have been few (if any) high-level reviews or recommendations focusing on the possibility of other high-impact respiratory pathogens with pandemic potential (p. 6)."

HIRPP calls for the improvement of national and global surveillance capacities on page 7, new surveillance technologies on page 8, and universal health care on page 9. On page 10, there is a call for social manipulation to assist them in achieving their aims: "Initial outreach and engagement with communities should occur before a disease outbreak so that strong existing relationships could be leveraged for good during response efforts... Social scientists should be consulted on potential community-level chokepoints, sites for cooperation, and meaningful reframing of public health objectives in locally relevant terms and practices."

"Countries need dedicated efforts to build public trust in local public health workforces (p. 10)." Such a need for trust in public health workforces was not previously an issue, but had been more or less implicit. The emphatic manner in which the authors of these documents obsess over gaining trust and not appearing coercive seems reminiscent of an abuser gaslighting a victim.

If we are dealing with a Hegelian dialectic, then mass vaccination was the goal to begin with (solution), and a pandemic situation (problem) was initiated to justify it (reaction). Page 11 states that "R&D [research and development] aimed at rapid vaccine development for novel threats and distributed surge manufacturing should be a top global pandemic planning priority... Nucleic acid (RNA and DNA)–based vaccines are widely seen as highly promising and potentially rapid vaccine development pathways, though they have not yet broken through with licensed products... Mass vaccination strategies should be developed and put in place to increase immediate access."

If you've been keeping up with the headlines, you've heard about edible vaccines by now. Research has been funded and is now currently underway to infuse lettuce and spinach with mRNA. The ultimate goal is to distribute mRNA in the food supply. Page 11 states, "The uptake of novel, needle-free administration technologies—specifically, those that enable either simplified or, potentially, self-administration—should be a priority to improve our collective ability to administer these countermeasures in clinically relevant timeframes."

HIRPP acknowledges certain non-pharmaceutical interventions like social distancing limit civil liberties and recommend that authorities produce enough data to justify their implementation: "WHO and national authorities will need to provide strong evidenced-backed reasoning for the necessity of NPIs in order to effectively implement them and to communicate their role and necessity to the public, especially for NPIs such as social distancing that inherently limit civil liberties. Therefore, they should undertake directly or support research on NPIs and disseminate their findings on these analyses."

Note that the recommendation is not to reference impartial research but rather for authorities to conduct or fund their own research to get the result they will need in order to better justify restricting human liberties.

I can't help but interpret this as directed at the United States funding gain-of-function research at the Wuhan lab: "Biosafety needs to become a national-level political priority, particularly for countries that are funding research with the potential to result in accidents with pathogens that could initiate a high-impact respiratory pandemic (p. 13)."

Figure 1: Potential Challenges Posed by High-Impact Respiratory Pathogens

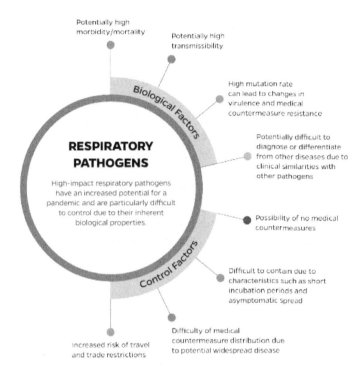

If I was going to create a pandemic situation based on data that is flimsy enough to be easily manipulated and tailored for public consumption, to be able to identify a virus everywhere or nowhere depending on my needs, I would use a respiratory pathogen based on the above statement, "Potentially difficult to diagnose or differentiate from other diseases due to clinical similarities with other pathogens."

Hence, the curious disappearance of the flu in 2020 and its replacement with COVID-19 which could be either identified or not identified based on the number of cycles run on a PCR test.

And now a reference to that convenient climate change narrative that can be used in any and every situation:

"Declining levels of protection from vaccines due to the influence of anti-vaccination sentiments in some communities is enabling previously declining respiratory viruses to cause significant outbreaks. Climate-related changes have altered the geography of habitats suitable for spread of certain pathogens and have changed patterns of migration, as humans move to escape consequences of extreme weather events. All of these factors increase the chance that new high-impact respiratory pathogens will emerge and spread, raising the possibility that an epidemic or pandemic will occur (p. 18)."

That one's a two-fer – climate change alarmism plus villainization of free-thinking people. On page 36 there is a section (box 5) that addresses another favorite globalist talking point entitled, *The Potential Problem of National Sovereignty in Pandemics*, thus demonstrating yet another motivation for why the NWO would choose a pandemic scenario for their Great Reset. It creates the perfect conditions for the centralization of global power in almost every way.

On page 47, HIRPP makes an argument for the importance of social sciences, that is, studying human behavior, in order to better persuade people to do as they're told. Propaganda is even more effective when everyone around you is buying into it. Later in the report (page 69) the example used for this social manipulation is that the Maori peoples' cultural values of solidarity, neighborliness, and mutual aid "can be leveraged for greater preparedness."

Sounds familiar, doesn't it? *Get vaccinated! Do it for your community!* Of course, the media was also instrumental in this public messaging (brainwashing). As stated on page 50, "Furthermore, these trusted partners may also act as advocates during times when public trust in public health is low and misinformation is rampant. Similarly, established and strong relationships with the news media can help to ensure the right messages get to members of the public."

HIRPP then gets to what this has always been about from the beginning: "Vaccination is the single most effective pharmaceutical intervention (p.51)," and then on page 52, "perhaps a coronavirus vaccine for an existing coronavirus could be used with some value for a novel coronavirus that causes high-impact respiratory outbreak."

But what kind of vaccines? Well, mRNA vaccines of course: "Nucleic acid vaccines, for example, are readily adapted for new targets by simply changing the nucleotide sequence; manufacture and its attendant safety testing is simplified because these vaccines could be considered "chemicals" and, like the manufacture of small-molecule chemical MCMs, may not need extensive batch testing once the manufacturing processes are established."

I appreciate that they got this all figured out just in time. To the credit of Johns Hopkins, they were at least honest here: "It is important to communicate to political leaders the absence of evidence surrounding many NPI interventions and the adverse consequences that may follow them."

The NPI, or non-pharmaceutical intervention they are most critical of is social distancing. "WHO should rapidly and clearly articulate its opposition to inappropriate NPIs, especially when they threaten public health response activities. Many NPIs, particularly those falling under social distancing, require support and acceptance by the public. As these measures inherently limit civil liberties by restricting individuals' movements, assembly, and social interaction, they can be a source of substantial opposition from affected individuals and populations (p. 73)."

I guess the WHO didn't listen to that one. The HIRPP then makes another recommendation that I appreciate – actually appreciate, not sarcastically – on page 75: "Life scientists working in high-containment or government laboratories are often required to undergo dual-use research of concern

(DURC) training; however, there are very few reporting mechanisms through which a concerned scientist can report the activities of a colleague to a superior without being worried about risking his or her career. There are even fewer clear mechanisms to connect the science and law enforcement communities if a scientist has substantial concerns that someone in her or his community is pursuing bioweapons development. A first step to cultivating this relationship is to create an appropriate and accessible method for life scientists and public health practitioners to report these kinds of concerns."

A dual-use technology is one that can be used as either a therapeutic or a weapon. Gene-editing technologies (which is what mRNA is) have been identified as dual use as they can be used as neuroweapons that could, according to some researchers, be more devastating than a nuclear war (think of a contagious neuroweapon).

I'm not sure if the globalist that had been writing the first 70 pages of the HIRPP got tired and a patriot took over to finish the final pages and include recommendations against useless NPI's and dangerous dual use research, or if these actually reasonable recommendations were included as preemptive damage control. Perhaps some clarity can be gained from the very beginning of the report on page 3: "This report was commissioned by and prepared for the Global Preparedness Monitoring Board. The opinions expressed in this publication are those of the authors. They do not purport to reflect the opinions, views or recommendations of the Global Preparedness Monitoring Board (GPMB),"

Next, we will look at the first annual report from the GPMB.

A World at Risk

A WORLD AT RISK

**Annual report on global preparedness
for health emergencies**

Global Preparedness Monitoring Board

September 2019

GPMB

A World at Risk is the first report completed by the Global Preparedness Monitoring Board (GPMB), which consists of 15 members, including Anthony Fauci, and was convened by the World Health Organization and World Bank Group in May of 2018 in response to Ebola outbreaks in 2016 and 2018 (Hegelian dialectic?). This first annual report was published in September of 2019 in preparation for a "high-impact respiratory pathogen pandemic".

The 2020 report is about what you would expect it to be – a drawn out see-I-told-you-so, a pandemic happened like we said it would, now give us more power so we can tell you what to do. The subsequent annual reports are reiterations of the same and are not worth including in this book for that reason. The more important thing to draw attention to is what was said about a high-impact respiratory pathogen pandemic just before that very thing occurred.

On page 4, the GPMB says of itself that it "complements and enhances existing accountability functions of the WHO, the UN, the World Bank, and other stakeholders" and that it challenges preparedness through the lens of governance, enhancing community engagement and trust, and preparing for and managing the fallout of a high-impact respiratory pathogen pandemic.

Immediately exposing itself as the work of the New World Order, the document demonizes and exaggerates population growth and climate change, "Disease amplifiers, including population growth and resulting strains on the environment, climate change, dense urbanization, exponential increases in international travel and migration, both forced and voluntary, increase the risk for everyone, everywhere (p. 6)."

Then they go on to demand obedience to the dictates of the IHR, which will be examined later in this book: "Heads of government in every country must commit to preparedness by implementing their binding obligations under the International

Health Regulations (IHR (2005)... G7, G20 and G77 Member States, and regional intergovernmental organizations must follow through on their political and funding commitments... (P. 7)."

At the top of page 8 is a command to establish a pandemic response leader, which in my view is likely the means by which they install their WHO puppets: "Heads of government must appoint a national high-level coordinator with authority and political accountability to lead whole-of-government and whole-of-society approaches."

Would this installed leader be Anthony Fauci in the United States? You know, the guy who in 2017 said that the Trump administration would face "a surprise outbreak." That statement alone coupled with the fact of his involvement in this high level report that narrowly precedes the thing it says will happen should raise more eyebrows than it does.

If the pandemic was planned, then it was planned to get "vaccines" into people. Further recommendations on page 8 include, "A rapidly spreading pandemic due to a lethal respiratory pathogen (whether naturally emergent or accidentally or deliberately released) poses additional preparedness requirements. Donors and multilateral institutions must ensure adequate investment in developing innovative vaccines and therapeutics, surge manufacturing capacity...".

Wherever large-scale vaccine operations are taking place you can find Bill Gates who comes from a family of depopulation advocates. "In 2017 Germany, India, Japan, Norway, the Bill & Melinda Gates Foundation, the Wellcome Trust and the World Economic Forum founded the Coalition for Epidemic Preparedness Innovations (CEPI) to facilitate focused support for vaccine development to combat major health epidemic/pandemic threats (p. 19)."

One of the "Ultimate Objectives" as included at the bottom of page 21 is that all countries submit to the globalist international health regulations: "All countries have reached full compliance with IHR (2005), have completed voluntary external or other independent assessments, and are objectively monitored by WHO on a regular basis to ensure continued improvement in preparedness. Recurrent national spending for preparedness is secured. Follow-up of countries' political and funding commitments made before G7, G20, G77 and regional organizations are monitored routinely."

As part of their "Progress to date" on page 23, the authors have included, "A number of Member States of the Commonwealth of Independent States Countries and those active in the European Environment and Sustainable Development Advisory Councils have increased their surveillance and laboratory capacities," and, "At the global level, the new Health Emergencies Programme established at the World Health Organization (WHO) following the 2014-2016 Ebola crisis in west Africa enabled the organization to take on a stronger, more effective operational role in outbreaks."

When a crisis results in the establishment of a globalist stronghold, there is reason to question whether the crisis was implemented by that stronghold in the first place as a means to get itself established. This Hegelian dialectic is a preferred social control strategy of authoritarians. The GPMB, a powerful organization, would not exist without the Ebola crisis in Africa. And if one is disinclined to accept that such crises can be manufactured, I refer the reader to the Tuskegee Experiments.

When documents like these tout a whole-of-government and whole-of-society system, they mean, "parties that must be engaged include national agencies beyond the health ministry, local governments, traditional and religious leaders, civil society, the research and security communities, the private sector, the media and operational experts (p.24)."

They can't do it alone. That's why propaganda is so necessary for them to achieve their aims. "Religious leader, civil society, the private sector" etc. must all be convinced to play along, but most importantly, women and girls: "Sustainable preparedness requires involvement of women and youth in planning and decision-making... It is important to ensure that the basic health needs of women and girls, including those for reproductive health, are met during an outbreak (p. 24)."

In other words, in all the chaos of a pandemic, let's not neglect our formerly most effective depopulation protocol, abortion, while we are working on our new favorite depopulation protocol, pandemics, which can be caused intentionally: "In addition to a greater risk of pandemics from natural pathogens, scientific developments allow for disease-causing microorganisms to be engineered or recreated in laboratories. Should countries, terrorist groups, or scientifically advanced individuals create or obtain and then use biological weapons that have the characteristics of a novel, high-impact respiratory pathogen, the consequences could be as severe as, or even greater, than those of a natural epidemic, as could an accidental release of epidemic-prone microorganisms (p.27)."

The GPMB complains that their "funding remains too low," and that there needs to be an improved capacity for "creating new vaccine manufacturing methods (p. 29)."

They seem to always be sure to mention nucleic acid type vaccines (such as mRNA). One of their "Ultimate Objectives" includes, "Distributed manufacturing of vaccines (including nucleic acid types) begins within days of obtaining the new sequences and effective vaccines are pre-tested and approved for use within weeks (p. 30)."

Funding for the GPMB's goals comes largely from the World Bank: "the World Bank Group, including IDA, has taken steps to develop not only financing, but the political support and coordination needed to build clinical research capacity in developing countries as a crucial component of global epidemic preparedness (p.32)."

But of course it's never enough and they go on to complain about being underfunded on the very next page. Naturally, they also call for greater global coordination: "While WHO leads the international response to any health emergency, it needs reliable, systematic backup from other United Nations agencies to address logistical and humanitarian developments that are beyond its scope to manage (p. 36)."

The final ultimate objective that the document closes with provides a good summary of their aims: "There is no ambiguity or delay in the United Nations systemwide response to a global health emergency. There are clear rules, roles and responsibilities, along with a designated leader, empowered with the authority to coordinate across the system and experienced in leading a global response through regular simulations or actual events. WHO can rapidly mobilize countries and partners early in an outbreak or health emergency (p. 39)."

Their ideal is to have a designated leader empowered with authority over nations to do whatever the UN deems necessary. Many nations, including the United States, appear to be on board with this idea as evidenced by their proposal to amend the International Health Regulations to cede more power to globalist organizations. At a minimum they appear to be privy to the same information because at the same time the GPMB was making their preparations for a high-impact respiratory pathogen pandemic, the US Department of Health and Human Services was doing the same with their Crimson Contagion exercise.

Crimson Contagion

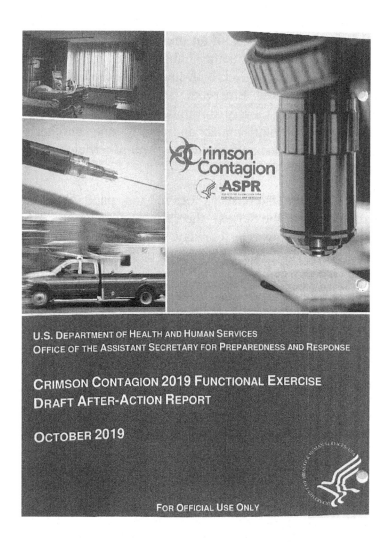

U.S. DEPARTMENT OF HEALTH AND HUMAN SERVICES
OFFICE OF THE ASSISTANT SECRETARY FOR PREPAREDNESS AND RESPONSE

CRIMSON CONTAGION 2019 FUNCTIONAL EXERCISE
DRAFT AFTER-ACTION REPORT

OCTOBER 2019

FOR OFFICIAL USE ONLY

Crimson Contagion is a functional exercise conducted by the US Department of Health and Human Services, the report being published in October of 2019. Before getting to the body of the text, it begins with an introduction that includes this statement that sheds some light on the goal of the exercise: "HHS and the U.S. Department of Homeland Security (DHS)/Federal Emergency Management Agency (FEMA) collaborated closely throughout the exercise in an effort to enhance their understanding of one another's operational capabilities and facilitate a more efficient and effective response to a pandemic."

A summary of the exercise is offered on page 5: "The culminating event of the Series—the Crimson Contagion 2019 Functional Exercise—was a four-day, multi-state, and multi-regional exercise that focused whole-of-community response and policy issues of workforce viability; critical infrastructure protection; economic impact; social distancing; scarce resource allocation; prioritization of vaccines and other countermeasures; available (or potentially available) funding streams or mechanisms to fund the response; and medical surge operations. The exercise began on August 13, 2019 and concluded on August 16, 2019."

The scenario overview of the exercise is offered on page 8: "The Crimson Contagion 2019 Functional Exercise scenario was based on a novel influenza A(H7N9) virus that originates in China and is antigenically distinct (not matched) from stockpiled H7N9 vaccines."

"The scenario starts off with tourists becoming ill in China with non-severe acute respiratory illness and then departing the Lhasa airport to other cities in China before flying back to their respective countries. During their flights home, additional tour group members, who were not ill when they embarked on their return flights from China, begin to experience the onset of respiratory symptoms and some develop fever."

Some of the findings of the exercise included:

- Inconsistent use of terminology regarding vaccine types and stockpiles caused confusion among response partners at all levels of government.

- HHS and DHS/FEMA's use of disparate information management systems hampered their ability to establish and maintain a national common operating picture.

- Both HHS and DHS/FEMA submitted senior leader briefs to the White House National Security Council during the exercise, which caused confusion regarding the official source of senior leader briefs.

- Response partners lack clarity on CDC's data sharing policies.

- State, local, tribal, and territorial partners were unclear on the kinds of information they needed to provide federal partners to address the full spectrum of community lifelines.

- HHS' regional staff lack clear guidance on the distribution of federal information management products to state and local partners.

- CDC's State Health Official and Regional Emergency Coordinator calls provided state partners with valuable insight into pandemic response activities at the national, regional, and state levels; however, the amount and types of information shared, as well as the existing limited mechanisms to share information were insufficient.

- Inconsistent use of terminology regarding vaccine types and stockpiles caused confusion among response partners at all levels of government.

- Some states were not clear on pre-pandemic vaccine or the Strategic National Stockpile asset distribution in response to an influenza pandemic.

- States questioned federal resource allocation decisions in response to an influenza pandemic.

- The distributed nature of school closure decisions caused confusion among exercise participants.

- The reasons for HHS' decision to halt seasonal influenza administration and distribution were unclear to state participants.

It doesn't sound like the exercise went well. But maybe that was the point. With such a lack of cohesion, a better case can be made for the necessity of installing a single pandemic response czar that is able to issue decrees without the strain and confusion of having to navigate the spiderweb of bureaucratic red tape.

The handling instructions on page ii seem a little extreme for an exercise simply meant to enhance the ability of the government to protect the American people: "Information gathered in this After-Action Report is designated as 'For Official Use Only' and should be handled as sensitive information that is not to be disclosed. This document should be safeguarded, handled, transmitted, and stored in accordance with appropriate security directives."

"At a minimum, the attached materials will be disseminated strictly on a need-to-know basis and, when unattended, will be stored in a locked container or area that offers sufficient protection against theft, compromise, inadvertent access, and unauthorized disclosure."

The "overarching exercise objectives" outlined on page 13 are as follows:

• Examine the ability of federal, state, and local governments, as well as private industry, nongovernmental organizations, and members of the public, to take coordinated protective actions during a pandemic influenza outbreak in accordance with applicable plans, policies, and procedures.

• Examine current gaps in capabilities and policies needed to determine risks to the affected population and the processes to manage, treat, and care for an overwhelming number of patients with an emphasis on people, pharmaceuticals, transportation requirements, and standards of care.

• Test and identity gaps in applicable plans, policies, and procedures to maintain a viable workforce in order to minimize disruptions to critical infrastructure systems and supply chains.

• Examine current mechanisms to integrate federal, state, and local decision-making and public messaging processes during a pandemic influenza response.

Anticipated hurdles in the coordination of pandemic response strategies are addressed on page 24, which I saw come to pass in my own experience: "Many of the hurdles stemmed from technology and equipment issues, including an uneven distribution of laptop computers and mobile devices among the workforce, user volume limitations on virtual private network systems, and insufficient internet bandwidth or connectivity."

Also manifested in many of our real-world experiences were the sanitation measures noted on page 29: "(e.g., mandatory wipe downs of desks, shared work spaces, phones, and key boards) and having security or other personnel perform a temperature check at the building entrances."

There were other strategies mentioned as well, such as the use of gloves, gowns, and facemasks. Ventilators were mentioned on page 22 in the context of resource allocation. But the focus of the exercise was primarily on there being no adequate mechanism for the Department of Health and Human Services to assume control as the federal agency leading the pandemic response.

So far we have seen that the Bill and Melinda Gates Foundation, the World Economic Forum, the Johns Hopkins Center for Health Security, and the Department of Health and Human Services all seem to have had a simultaneous premonition of a significantly disruptive pandemic event, but NTI, Georgetown University, and the Center for Global Development all had the same premonition strangely enough, so they put their heads together to explore how best to manage a response to a deliberate biological event.

A Spreading Plague: Lessons and Recommendations for Responding to a Deliberate Biological Event

This is a report published by The Nuclear Threat Initiative (NTI) in June of 2019. You may recall that the list of anti-human depopulation quotations at the beginning of this book includes a quote from Ted Turner, leading investor of the NTI: "A total world population of 250-300 million people, a 95% decline from present levels, would be ideal."

The cover page of the report summarizes the tabletop exercise: "On the eve of the 2019 Munich Security Conference, senior leaders from security, public health, humanitarian, and political sectors participated in a dramatic tabletop exercise designed to explore global capability to rapidly respond to a deliberate biological event."

The report begins with a warning that "the risks of a global catastrophic biological event are growing (p. 2)," and that, "the lack of established procedures would very likely undermine the trust and cooperation needed between the health professionals, humanitarian responders, and security officials who would be aiming for a coordinated, effective international response (p. 2)."

So the goal of the report is to establish procedures in hopes of increasing public trust. The description they provide of the exercise is that it is a "tabletop exercise designed to explore command, control, and coordination of an international response to an unusual and rapidly spreading biological event that began in the fictional country of "Vestia." The dramatic exercise uncovered major gaps in international coordination, information sharing, and attribution between health and security officials. It sparked disagreements among leading experts over whether a permanent United Nations-based coordinator is needed to facilitate coordination among the various entities responsible for pandemic response (p. 2)."

Here again we see the push toward installing a central UN leader that would require the diminishing of national powers. On page 3, the report includes a warning offered by Bill Gates at the 2017 Munich Security Conference: "We ignore the link between health security and international security at our own peril."

The group of "18 senior security, public health, and humanitarian leaders convened to respond to the fast-spreading plague that began in Vestia as a way to further explore known gaps in global preparedness to respond to a high-consequence, genetically engineered agent and to identify ways to close those gaps (p. 3)."

One of the things they learned is that if a government wanted to commit an act of terror, the lack of coordination between investigative agencies would make it easier to get away with: "...mechanisms for coordination and communication among UNODA, national and regional investigative teams, and INTERPOL have not been well defined for situations that have the potential to include both terrorist and state involvement (p. 7)."

Page 10 offers another plug for a centralized locus of power: "...sovereign countries that ultimately have a lot of power to decide whether to report or to allow investigation into an outbreak that is spreading within and beyond its borders may not be as cooperative."

Therefore, of course, there should be a UN dictator to ensure cooperation as recommended on page 11: "The Office of the United Nations Secretary-General should designate a permanent facilitator...".

Another recommendation is that, "The UNSG and the WHO Director General should co-convene a meeting in 2020 to propose specific mechanisms to enable the rapid exchange of genetic information across sectors during a deliberate biological event and other high-consequence scenarios (p. 13)."

Perhaps they are relying on the chaos and confusion that ensues following a global pandemic event in order to obscure the true cause: "There is no question that world leaders will quickly call for an investigation into the source of a spreading deliberate biological attack to identify the perpetrator(s) and deter further use. However, the source of an attack could be unknown and difficult to determine during an already confusing and globally spreading outbreak, and it is unclear which organization(s) would have the resources, workforce, and protocols to lead the security-related investigation—particularly if the source of the attack remains unclear for any length of time (p. 15)."

Findings of the report suggest:

- Better global biosurveillance capabilities are required to drive data, advance analytics, and forecast outbreak spread.

- UN Member States should prioritize financing for the WHO Health Emergencies Programme.

- In 2019 and 2020, international organizations, including the WHO, UNODA, and the World Economic Forum, should convene private sector companies to identify gaps and concrete next steps…

The NTI reports are relatively brief and I include them here only to demonstrate certain key items such as the timing of events and their alignment with other documents of apparently disparate authorship. The following document, however, is of the same authorship, but it offers at least one point that makes it unique which is worth spending some time on.

Strengthening Global Systems to Prevent and Respond to High-Consequence Biological Threats

NTI Paper

NOVEMBER 2021

Strengthening Global Systems to Prevent and Respond to High-Consequence Biological Threats

Results from the 2021 Tabletop Exercise Conducted in Partnership with the Munich Security Conference

SUMMARY

In March 2021, NTI partnered with the Munich Security Conference to conduct a tabletop exercise on reducing high-consequence biological threats. The exercise examined gaps in national and international biosecurity and pandemic preparedness architectures—exploring opportunities to improve prevention and response capabilities for high-consequence biological events. This report summarizes the exercise scenario, key findings from the discussion, and actionable recommendations for the international community.

A post-pandemic report from the Nuclear Threat Initiative, this paper shares the findings of a tabletop exercise conducted in March of 2021 that purported to reduce high-consequence biological threats. In the forward, the authors state that, "the next global catastrophe could be caused by the deliberate misuse of the tools of modern biology or by a laboratory accident (p. 4)."

Are we not still calling the Wuhan lab leak a conspiracy theory? I believe I had been informed that biolabs are extraordinarily secure and "laboratory accidents" do not occur. But just in case such a thing is now possible, we need to be proactive: "We cannot afford to be reactive. We must build our public health and medical systems to be anticipatory, responding energetically and proactively in the face of uncertainty (p. 4)."

Amendments to the IHR (2005) being proposed include a proactive approach as well. The idea is that the WHO should have authority to declare public health emergencies before they even occur. Just in case. Think, "preventative lockdowns".

The tabletop scenario is described on page 6: "The exercise scenario portrayed a deadly, global pandemic involving an unusual strain of monkeypox virus that emerged in the fictional nation of Brinia and spread globally over 18 months. Ultimately, the exercise scenario revealed that the initial outbreak was caused by a terrorist attack using a pathogen engineered in a laboratory with inadequate biosafety and biosecurity provisions and weak oversight. By the end of the exercise, the fictional pandemic resulted in more than three billion cases and 270 million fatalities worldwide."

Before introducing Figure 1 on page 10, I would like to remind the reader of the dates surrounding the Monkeypox scare of 2022.

Idaho murder victim
Kaylee Goncalves had
moved out of home…

Family of American
dying in UAE prison
rips Biden admin for…

17-year-old scolded for
crying over
transgender woman's…

NEWS

First case of monkeypox confirmed in US this year in man who had traveled to Canada

By Patrick Reilly

May 18, 2022 | 6:30pm | Updated

The first case in 2022 in the United States occurred Mid-May. Now look at the "fictional" timeline included on page 10 of the NTI's **2021** report and note the date of the first attack.

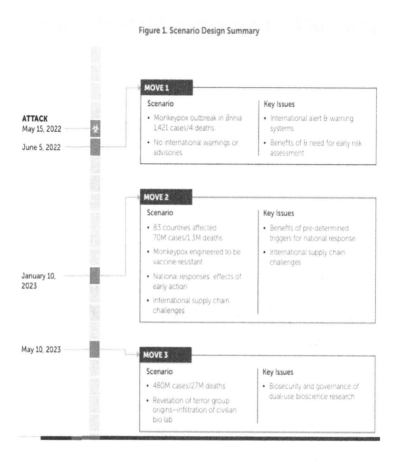

Figure 1. Scenario Design Summary

Page 11 states that, "Because monkeypox is not naturally found in Brinia, local and international experts consider this outbreak to be unusual" just as it is not naturally found in the United States commonly and should also be considered unusual. On the same page, a fictional group of countries "have prioritized keeping their economies open, undertaking little-to-no NPIs, and downplaying the virus and its potential impacts. These countries have experienced much worse outcomes in terms of illness and mortality," a somber imaginary lesson about how not taking the authorities seriously when they are attempting one of their routine health scares will likely result in mass casualties.

In the exercise, "Brinian intelligence reveals that the engineered monkeypox virus was developed illicitly at the fictional country of Arnica's leading institute for virology. Arnica (population 75 million) has a history of conflict with neighboring Brinia (see map in Figure 5). An independent Arnican terrorist group—the SPA—had worked with sympathetic laboratory scientists to engineer a highly contagious, deadly pathogen and disperse it at crowded train stations in Brinia during the national holiday, when much of the population was travelling domestically and internationally. The SPA had exploited the Arnican government's weak oversight of its bioscience research laboratories. SPA sympathizers working in Arnica's leading virology institute used publicly available scientific publications to guide their work to modify the monkeypox virus to make it more transmissible and resistant to currently available vaccines (p. 13)."

It is noted on page 14 that in this exercise, "the scenario arguably depicted a "best case" where the country of origin reported what it knew to the WHO in a timely manner and welcomed international investigation," but even then, the results were dire. Many participants "stressed that the international community requires a more coordinated international biosurveillance network, which also incorporates pathogen genome sequencing."

On page 15, a case seems to be made for inflating the initial fatality rate: "One participant observed that the number of fatalities would not be a good measure to track in the early period of a pandemic because it is a lagging indicator at a time of exponential growth in cases."

Of constant concern to these people is the question of whether the people are obeying their governments:

"Another consideration is the strength of the country's public health system and whether the population is reducing the risk of spread by using NPIs and avoiding mass gatherings (p. 15)."

"One participant noted that formally shifting the WHO PHEIC [Public Health Emergency of International Concern] to a graded system might require a change to the IHR (2005), which could pose significant political challenges (p. 15)."

As I write these words, our globalist overlords are meeting to discuss matters such as the one noted above. Amendments to the IHR (2005) are currently being drafted.

Further on page 15, there is a call for transparency. I would say *the illusion of transparency* is what they mean, "Deliberations that currently occur behind closed doors—the WHO Emergency Committee, for example—would benefit if, at a minimum, an outside expert group could analyze the data and reach conclusions in parallel."

Probably needless to say, but there are no "outside expert groups" in this realm. All of the science has been settled within the confines of globalist dogma, and if a real expert dares contradict said "science" they are ostracized and wouldn't be allowed even to voice their opinion on social media, much less be allowed to scrutinize data from the WHO.

We can know one thing for certain. These tabletop exercises are not scientific at all, but rather mere exercises in how better to control people. For instance, we know by demonstration that mask mandates and avoiding social gatherings had no impact on COVID-19, yet the same nonsense continues to be regurgitated in these reports, such as, "NPIs such as mask mandates and ceasing mass gatherings were deemed to be critical for blocking chains of disease transmission (p. 17)."

Report recommendations beginning on page 22:

- The NTI-MSC tabletop exercise and other studies have made a compelling case that a radically strengthened global biosurveillance system is needed.

- Risk gradations should be built explicitly on thresholds of pandemic potential—i.e., the potential of a disease outbreak to spread globally and yield high case counts—as well as estimated severity, such as case fatality rate.

- A joint assessment mechanism is needed.

- Governments should take anticipatory action.

- Triggered actions should include a range of NPIs, including proactive social distancing and mask-wearing guidelines, and large-scale testing and contact tracing.

Appendix B on page 31 wraps up the document with a plug for aggressive lockdowns. Would any other conclusion be drawn in a globalist document?

R= the basic reproductive number of the virus:

"The "Moderate" response countries open up in January, increasing R to approximately 2.2, before locking down in the summer of 2023 when the outbreak is undeniable. Finally, the "Effective" response countries lock down aggressively in February 2023 and keep R below 1 throughout the remainder of the exercise."

To summarize, we need aggressive lockdowns, we need the WHO to have more power, we need a fake independent agency to corroborate the WHO's claims and make them appear as though they're transparent, we need to impose changes now in anticipation of future events, and when an event does occur, we'll need widespread monitoring and various freedom-restricting government dictates.

So far, we have seen involvement from the World Economic Forum, the Johns Hopkins Center for Health Security, the Department of Health and Human Services, the Nuclear Threat Initiative, Georgetown University, and the Center for Global Development in the creation of these timely pandemic drills. Before moving on to other items, there is one more pandemic exercise to review, this one from the U.S. Naval War College.

Urban Outbreak 2019

U.S. NAVAL WAR COLLEGE
Est. 1884
NEWPORT RHODE ISLAND

Urban Outbreak 2019
Pre-Analytic "Quick Look"

Benjamin Davies, Heath Brightman, Jacob Brostuen, David Polatty and Brittany Card

A product of the Civilian-Military Humanitarian Response Program,
United States Naval War College

October 31, 2019

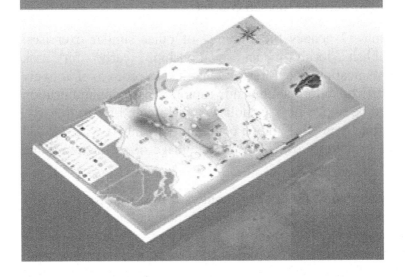

Page 1 of the exercise provides this overview of Urban Outbreak: "The document references "Urban Outbreak 2019," which was an analytic war game designed, delivered and analyzed by NWC's Humanitarian Response Program in collaboration with Uniformed Services University of the Health Sciences (USUHS) - National Center for Disaster Medicine and Public Health (NCDMPH) and Johns Hopkins University's Applied Physics Lab. In September 2019, Urban Outbreak brought together 50 experts from five different sectors who averaged 10 years of humanitarian response experience. Over two days they gamed an infectious disease outbreak response in a notional but realistic city with a population of 21 million people."

The first move of the exercise according to the "Pre-Analytic Quick Look" of Urban Outbreak "introduced the outbreak of a pathogen that was originally identified in rodents but is later spread by person to person contact."

Finding #7 echoes the findings of other similar exercises: "Establish local media relationships early for risk communication as outbreak intensifies. In order to effectively combat misinformation and rumors, risk communication should be hyper-local, establish a track record for truth early, and directly involve known community members with a stated focus of honesty over polished language or production value (p. 2)."

"Any containment strategy requires testing and tracing. This is not possible once a large enough population is infected. In the same way, altering business, social or cultural practices is significantly less effective when a society is facing a wide range of new challenges, especially severe economic and social pressures. Clarity, speed, and repetition are essential for changes within a population and are most effectively achieved before other factors start making decisions for them (p. 3)."

Coercing people into compliance is more effective than forcing them into it: "Sick people actively seeking care, testing, and public health messages concerning self-isolation and quarantine of contacts are the ways to end outbreaks. Forced mass quarantines are a direct barrier to those activities. One cannot slow the spread of disease if people hide infections out of fear or stigma. When authorities attempt to enforce a mass quarantine on a large population, they will not be 100% effective. By stigmatizing the infection and symptoms they will teach others to hide their symptoms and drive key populations underground. This results in less sharing of information with authorities and medical providers, and the most desperate and the highest risk populations will seek to break quarantine (p. 4)."

How to coerce people into compliance was explored as well: "Upon reaching the apex of the outbreak in round two, NGO's and some U.S. Government (USG) independently identified a shift from national to local media outlets and dissemination, focusing on TV, radio, and billboards for "carpet bombing" public health messaging (as opposed to web, national, or international) in order to build local trust, relevance, and community response rate. It will also increase a responder's control over speed of delivery and accuracy (p. 5)."

The report encourages "authenticity and truth" on page 5, stating that, "In a sustained crisis, the public will become increasingly dismissive of messages that don't reflect the immediacy or intensity of their experience or sentiments," so don't piss on the people's shoes and tell them it's raining, in other words. One might think being truthful would be a given, but perhaps people in government will lie by default unless otherwise directed.

One thing learned from the exercise is that the participants blindly accepted the information they were given, which surprised the game designers: "Designers anticipated questions about data collection and reliability by such a wide array of seasoned experts but not blind acceptance of such abnormal reports (p. 5)."

There were additional areas of inquiry listed in Appendix III that were not discussed in greater detail in the report. These included:

- Loss of power, utilities, dockworkers, security, etc.

- Increased international military role

- Quarantine/roadblocks

- Security – rise of gangs and religious groups

Those particular topics would have likely been enlightening to read about in more detail. Maybe there is a reason they were left out of the report aside from being casually mentioned at the end.

Many of the documents we have thus far reviewed pertained to the anticipation of a pandemic event that then occurred shortly after their publication, defying all probability. Next, we will explore another abomination from Johns Hopkins Center for Health Security, this one demonstrating one of the motivations for inciting the Reset pandemic in the first place: to institute Orwellian measures to eradicate free speech.

National Priorities to Combat Misinformation and Disinformation for COVID-19 and Future Public Health Threats: A Call for a National Strategy

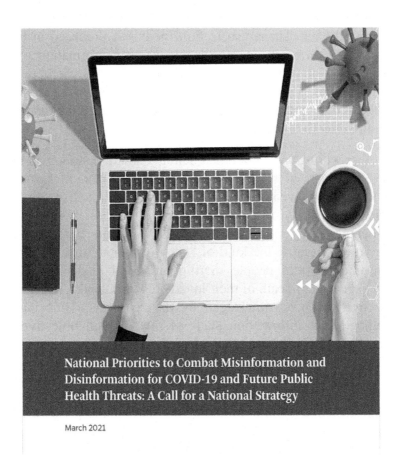

National Priorities to Combat Misinformation and Disinformation for COVID-19 and Future Public Health Threats: A Call for a National Strategy

March 2021

JOHNS HOPKINS
BLOOMBERG SCHOOL
of PUBLIC HEALTH

Center for
Health Security

Blatantly unconstitutional, this document from the Johns Hopkins Center for Health Security advocates for securing complete control of the narrative and penalizing any who express dissent. Their justification for this is premised in the executive summary: "health-related misinformation or disinformation can lead to more infections, deaths, disruption, and disorganization of the effort... disinformation can lead to a range of outcomes that have national security implications and require effective response."

In other words, unprogrammed beliefs that are not allowed by the state pose a threat to our national security. In fact, if people are allowed to share their opinions, it will result in other people dying, even if those opinions have been authenticated by empirical evidence. We know this is what they mean because the kind of "disinformation" that is being censored includes people sharing on social media that the official cause of death of their loved one was the vaccine. This has even been acknowledged by the censorers. They have admitted that information such as this, though objectively true, "violates community standards" (or some such rhetoric) because it could result in vaccine hesitancy.

The first video that was removed on my YouTube channel, Deconstructing a Paradigm, was one that simply presented a report by Pfizer themselves. To present a document and read what it says verbatim is an objective truth, yet it contradicted the narrative so it was removed. In short, the objective truth is now against the rules and will not be tolerated.

The words "disinformation" and "misinformation" could in many places be replaced with "the truth" throughout this document for a better understanding of what we are really up against. Try it! "The truth can lead to a range of outcomes that have national security implications and require effective response."

The executive summary goes on to identify the United States Constitution as part of the problem: "Constitutional concerns with free speech limit some potential interventions."

Reading forward, it should be noted that many of the things deemed "misinformation" at one time have now been proven true and have been accepted into the mainstream narrative, such as that the vaccine does not prevent a person from being infected with COVID-19. That fact was once disinformation and you would be banned on social media for saying it, but now it has been codified into their narrative for why you need a booster shot.

Nevertheless, they are adamant about what a monumental problem it is that people be allowed to say what they can observe with their own eyes. "There is an urgent national security and public health need to ensure effective management of public health misinformation and disinformation (executive summary)."

You shared a meme of a sheep wearing a facemask? Yeah, that's a matter of national security. And they aren't just coming after the information itself, they're coming after the people who dare speak freely and share it. Pillar 1 in the executive summary is, "Intervene against false and damaging content as well as the sources propagating it."

And they mean what they say. Alex Jones was deplatformed and demonetized in an attempt to silence him, and when that didn't work because he had built his own operation, they came after him via a weaponized judiciary. That is only one example of many.

This document provides an exemplary demonstration of the propensity for dishonesty in these globalist agencies. Anyone that isn't naïve as a 5-year-old can see through such laughable statements as their stated desire to "establish a national non-partisan commission that provides neutral, evidence-based guidance" regarding COVID-19. I have not once seen anything remotely neutral in regard to this. It is always one-sided propaganda. The same is true of their "fact-checking" strategy: "Improve resources for public verification of questionable content through the development of a robust fact-checking infrastructure with support, training, and guiding principles for fact-checking organizations (p. iv)." Is it still considered fact-checking when it is facts that they are seeking to omit?

Page v of the executive summary enumerates the litany of alphabet soup agencies enlisted for the war on truth: "Increase coordination across the range of government stakeholders and conduct a cross-governmental analysis of efforts and responsibilities for managing health-related misinformation and disinformation in order to streamline and organize efforts. Key US agencies include the Department of Defense, Department of Health and Human Services, and Department of Homeland Security as well as intelligence agencies such as the Federal Bureau of Investigation, the National Security Agency, and the Central Intelligence Agency."

The DOD, DHS, FBI, NSA, and CIA? That is the kind of response I would expect if we were invaded by hostile aliens. The introduction on page 1 attempts to justify why such a response is necessary: "False information, intentional or not, has had a myriad of effects in the past year, including reduced trust in public health responders, increased belief in false medical cures, and politicization of public health measures. The spread of these falsehoods has led to more infections, deaths, disruption, and disorganization of the effort to combat the pandemic."

This is supposed to be a novel virus, isn't it? Then how can they know which medical cures are "false"? There hasn't been enough time to demonstrate efficacy of any kind of treatment, let alone vaccines, after only about a year (this document was published March 2021). Also impossible to demonstrate, is that "the spread of these falsehoods has led to more infections and deaths". Can we get a fact-check on that? No? Ok, well if we allow that, then doesn't it also follow that preventing people from telling others about the deaths of their loved ones due to vaccines has led to more infections and deaths? The hypocrisy is astounding.

Health-related misinformation and disinformation is defined on page 1 as "messages that contradict the best expert evidence available." One might wonder "best expert evidence" as determined by whom? According to the likes of Johns Hopkins University, Greta Thunberg is a climate expert while world-renowned climatologists are declared guilty of disinformation.

Page 2: "In February 2020, the World Health Organization (WHO) characterized the overwhelming amount of COVID-19 information—both true and untrue—as an "infodemic, which undermines public health measures and leads to unnecessary loss of life"... However, major efforts have been made since WHO declared a COVID-19 infodemic, including the release of a research agenda for managing infodemics," or for Orwell fans, The Ministry of Truth has been established.

No dystopian future is complete without a Ministry of Truth or artificial intelligence: "Many current recommendations focus on education and "inoculation" against misinformation, more accountability on the part of social media platforms in identifying and controlling the misinformation messages, interagency and international cooperation in managing misinformation, and use of machine learning/ artificial intelligence to help identify and flag misinformation and disinformation in real time. In response to misinformation and disinformation that has spread via traditional news media, private groups have begun efforts to deter advertising with news organizations that are perpetuating misinformation. Policy recommendations and legislative bills have been developed in an attempt to fight misinformation and disinformation (p. 3)."

"Facebook has also created the Oversight Board to review content removal. The WhatsApp and Facebook Messenger misinformation policies center on preventing the spread of viral messages by limiting the number of times a message can be forwarded, labeling forwarded messages, and using machine learning to recognize and remove accounts that are sending out mass messages. Google-owned YouTube's medical misinformation strategy does not allow information contradictory to that of local health authorities or WHO... In one of the earliest efforts to combat false information about vaccines, Pinterest began limiting and breaking the search function for vaccine-related information on the platform (p. 4)."

That shouldn't be surprising since Mark Zuckerberg admitted that Facebook colluded with the FBI to interfere with the 2020 election and the Musk vs. Twitter situation revealed that the majority of Twitter traffic are bots designed to direct the narrative. The strategies listed in the above paragraph are just those they're willing to openly acknowledge.

The "key stakeholders critical to successful misinformation and disinformation management" according to Johns Hopkins University include social media platform owners and operators, news media organizations and journalists, governments, policy makers, national security organizations, and public health agencies and institutions. The extent to which they call for government involvement is alarming as they praise governments for, "developing fact-checking government run websites, passing legislation punishing perpetrators for spreading false information, and instituting national or international government- or police-led surveillance of reported alleged misinformation or disinformation (p. 6)."

Have you seen those videos of people getting arrested and pulled out of their homes for sharing disinformation (telling the truth) online in Australia, Canada, Germany, and other countries? That is what this document calls for. That is the New World Order they would like implemented – one in which free speech is dead.

On page 8 there is a paragraph that summarizes their priorities for a national strategy: "The COVID-19 pandemic has demonstrated the need for a national strategy to combat health-related misinformation and disinformation. Policymakers should act now, while the threat is clear and before conditions worsen, to create such a strategy. This will require a broad approach organized by 4 principles or conceptual pillars: (1) intervene against false and damaging content as well as the sources propagating it, (2) promote and ensure the abundant presence and dissemination of factual information, (3) increase the public's resilience to misinformation and disinformation, and (4) ensure a whole-of-nation response through multisector and multiagency collaboration."

My interpretation is as follows:

(1) intervene against false and damaging content as well as the sources propagating it – *eradicate free speech*

(2) promote and ensure the abundant presence and dissemination of factual information – *disseminate propaganda*

(3) increase the public's resilience to misinformation and disinformation – *brainwash the public*

(4) ensure a whole-of-nation response through multisector and multiagency collaboration – *ensure there are no dissenters*

Johns Hopkins is not recommending the involvement of government agencies without their cooperation. The government is already complicit: "Both the Worldwide Threat Assessment, completed by the Director of National Intelligence, and the Homeland Threat Assessment, completed by DHS, have noted the threat of influence and disinformation campaigns, including in the context of COVID-19… The DOD, DOS, and intelligence agencies monitoring this information space should coordinate more closely with the press and other communication partners, including social media platform companies to expose information threats and increase public vigilance against these efforts (p. 9)."

Because of Zuckerberg's loose lips we know that the government certainly has been influencing social media, and we know from congressional hearings from decades ago that the CIA controls the mainstream media. Still, more government involvement is called for: "Coordination between government and social media companies may be needed to monitor newly emerging platforms as they grow (p. 9)."

Are you involved in a newly emerging platform? If so, you're being watched. And I would wager that if you have even a modicum of influence on social media, you're being watched there as well.

Page 10 states, "Currently, there is a lack of consensus and understanding on how to best control infodemics while also respecting freedom of speech and avoiding abuses of power from authorities. Actions should aim to align with principles and guidance outlined by international stakeholders, including the United Nations and WHO."

Why the UN and the WHO? Because they operate unimpeded by the Constitution.

The need for increased funding for propaganda is made known on page 11: "Rapidly available funding to establish advertising campaigns during public health emergencies to help increase dissemination and volume of accurate information are needed. For instance, the Ad Council has recently launched a $50 million campaign to increase uptake of the vaccine."

On page 12 there is a call to infiltrate trusted members of the community since they know the government trashed their own reputation long ago: "A notable proportion of the population may have limited trust in official government sources and may seek information from more trusted community partners, such as religious leaders, medical care providers, or local community organizers. While the federal government should work to depoliticize health-related messaging, it should also seek to develop additional avenues to provide information to the public through trusted messengers."

Page 12 states that institutional communication teams should work with the news media to "assist them in pushing back on false information. This is especially important for reaching new audiences, that may be more skeptical of public health interventions, through local news and conservative news sources."

Based on that, we know what they mean when referencing "political affiliations" and "ideological values". Reading between the lines, it is the Christians and Conservatives who are deemed most likely to push back against medical tyranny. "Ideological values, political affiliations, and other aspects of identity can play a substantial role in a person's exposure to information as well as their willingness to believe or reject misinformation. A national strategy should outline avenues for the establishment of programs from a range of sources, including news media, schools, communities, and social media, to help improve public understanding of how to discern trustworthy information sources, detect hallmarks of disinformation, and find accurate resources."

So they will control the narrative through the news media, schools, communities, and social media – all the major social mechanisms for information control except Hollywood, though perhaps the involvement of Hollywood is so overt at this point that they didn't bother to mention it.

It appears that the COVID-19 crisis was just the thing the globalists needed to begin eradicating free speech, which is a prerequisite for the New World Order. If they didn't plan the pandemic, they must have just gotten lucky. But of course, they did plan it because that is what the entire Great Reset hinges on.

Interim Operational Considerations for Implementing the Shielding Approach to Prevent COVID-19 Infections in Humanitarian Settings

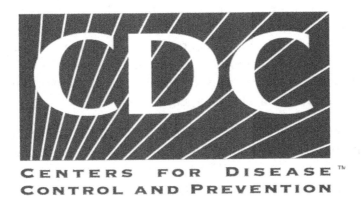

Interim Operational Considerations for Implementing the Shielding Approach to Prevent COVID-19 Infections in Humanitarian Settings

This document presents considerations from the perspective of the U.S. Centers for Disease Control & Prevention (CDC) for implementing the shielding approach in humanitarian settings as outlined in guidance documents focused on camps, displaced populations and low-resource settings.[1,2] This approach has never been documented and has raised questions and concerns among humanitarian partners who support response activities in these settings. The purpose of this document is to highlight potential implementation challenges of the shielding approach from CDC's perspective and guide thinking around implementation in the absence of empirical data. Considerations are based on current evidence known about the transmission and severity of coronavirus disease 2019 (COVID-19) and may need to be revised as more information becomes available. Please check the CDC website periodically for updates.

#EXZM Is ExZACKly What You Need To Hear!
www.exzacktamountas.com

What is the Shielding Approach[1]?

The shielding approach aims to reduce the number of severe COVID-19 cases by limiting contact between individuals at higher risk of developing severe disease ("high-risk") and the general population ("low-risk"). High-risk individuals would be temporarily relocated to safe or "green zones" established at the household, neighborhood, camp/sector or community level depending on the context and setting.[1,2] They would have minimal contact with family members and other low-risk

Many people seem to regard the idea that at some point, Americans may be put into FEMA camps as one of the more outlandish conspiracy theories on the market. But all throughout history, nations rise and fall. There have been camps in recent history and people are dying in camps in China right now. So of course there is nothing outlandish about the idea of camps at all. Especially not now as we have seen them erected in many different parts of the world under the auspices of a health emergency.

Here we have yet another situation arising from the pandemic that conveniently contributes to the NWO. Must be another coincidence that COVID-19 just so happens to assist the globalists in executing all their goals.

There are not, to the best of my knowledge, people in camps in America at present (though there are innocent people in prison), but COVID-19 has served as a precedent to lay the infrastructure for it when the next pandemic hits, which we are assured by Bill Gates WILL be happening. Vast complexes have been built in other parts of the world. They didn't go to all that trouble just to never use those facilities again. The CDC suggests something they call "the shielding approach".

In this document, updated in July of 2020, the CDC does not shy away from the term, "camps", but rather use it openly while dressing it up in the appearance of a humanitarian motivation: "This document presents considerations from the perspective of the U.S. Centers for Disease Control & Prevention (CDC) for implementing the shielding approach in humanitarian settings as outlined in guidance documents focused on camps, displaced populations, and low-resource settings."

In the next paragraph on page one, they summarize what the shielding approach is: "The shielding approach aims to reduce the number of severe COVID-19 cases by limiting contact between individuals at higher risk of developing severe disease ("high-risk") and the general population ("low-risk"). High-risk individuals would be temporarily relocated to safe or "green zones" established at the household, neighborhood, camp/sector or community level depending on the context and setting. They would have minimal contact with family members and other low-risk residents."

They further warn that "implementation of the approach necessitates strict adherence to protocol." There will need to be personnel to ensure compliance.

Table 1: Summary of the Shielding Approach[1]

Level	Movement/ Interactions
Household (HH) Level: A specific room/area designated for high-risk individuals who are physically isolated from other HH members.	Low-risk HH members should not enter the green zone. If entry is necessary, it should be done only by healthy individuals after washing hands and using face coverings. Interactions should be at a safe distance (approx. 2 meters). Minimum movement of high-risk individuals outside the green zone. Low-risk HH members continue to follow social distancing and hygiene practices outside the house.
Neighborhood Level: A designated shelter/group of shelters (max 5-10 households), within a small camp or area where high-risk members are grouped together. Neighbors "swap" households to accommodate high-risk individuals.	Same as above
Camp/Sector Level: A group of shelters such as schools, community buildings within a camp/sector (max 50 high-risk individuals per single green zone) where high-risk individuals are physically isolated together.	One entry point is used for exchange of food, supplies, etc. A meeting area is used for residents and visitors to interact while practicing physical distancing (2 meters). No movement into or outside the green zone.

"Camp" is described as, "A group of shelters such as schools, community buildings within a camp/sector (max 50 high-risk individuals per single green zone) where high-risk individuals are physically isolated together… One entry point is used for exchange of food, supplies, etc. A meeting area is used for residents and visitors to interact while practicing physical distancing (2 meters). No movement into or outside the green zone (p. 2)."

The Shielding Approach uses existing facilities and homes that are simply cordoned off and supervised which are then referred to as green zones. There is no need to use funds to build new infrastructure. Almost anywhere can be a green zone with some minor adjustments: "The shielding approach advises against any new facility construction to establish green zones; however, few settings will have existing shelters or communal facilities with designated latrines/bathing facilities to accommodate high-risk individuals. In these settings, most latrines used by HHs (households) are located outside the home and often shared by multiple HHs."

The table beginning on page 1 breaks the shielding approach down into three levels: the household level (HH), the neighborhood level, and the camp/sector level. The neighborhood level is described as: "A designated shelter/group of shelters (max 5-10 households), within a small camp or area where high-risk members are grouped together. Neighbors "swap" households to accommodate high-risk individuals."

This cannot be done without forcibly overthrowing a neighborhood. Perhaps they use words like "latrine" instead of bathroom because this is clearly a military operation. They come into your home, pull some of your family members out and replace them with strangers, disrupting family units, and if you don't like it that's too bad, because you'll be fenced in and there will be armed guards to ensure "strict adherence to protocol": "Monitoring protocols will need to be developed for each type of green zone… Dedicated staff need to be identified to monitor each green zone. Monitoring includes both adherence to protocols and potential adverse effects or outcomes due to isolation and stigma. It may be necessary to assign someone within the green zone, if feasible, to minimize movement in/out of green zones (p. 3)."

Don't get your hopes up thinking you could use a vacation like this. This is a labor camp, they plan on putting you to work: "To minimize external contact, each green zone should include able-bodied high-risk individuals capable of caring for residents who have disabilities or are less mobile. Otherwise, designate low-risk individuals for these tasks, preferably who have recovered from confirmed COVID-19 and are assumed to be immune."

Note that the people in these camps are not necessarily infected. These are healthy people who have just been designated "high risk" or "low risk" and have been contained by their government. They realize people might not be too happy about being imprisoned: "Isolation/separation from family members, loss of freedom and personal interactions may require additional psychosocial support structures/systems (p. 3)."

On page 4, the CDC recommends planning for a duration of at least 6 months. Considering what "two weeks to flatten the curve" turned into, I'm thinking 6 months really means years.

We have seen careful attention paid to the "appearance of coercion" in these globalist documents, and the CDC's shielding approach is no different: "While the shielding approach is not meant to be coercive, it may appear forced or be misunderstood in humanitarian settings."

It doesn't appear forced, it is forced. The whole premise of the shielding approach is to put people into camps and force their compliance: "Compliance and behavior change are the primary rate-limiting steps and may be driven by social and emotional factors. These changes are difficult in developed, stable settings; thus, they may be particularly challenging in humanitarian settings which bring their own set of multi-faceted challenges that need to be taken into account (p. 5)."

Rest assured, they will be taking your compliance into account! And they fully anticipate pushback: "This shielding approach may have an important psychological impact and may lead to significant emotional distress... Separating families and disrupting and deconstructing multigenerational households may have long-term negative consequences (p. 5)."

I don't see why anyone should be bothered by having their neighborhood turned into a prison camp. For example, what could go wrong with house swapping? "Households participating in house swaps or sector-wide cohorting are at particular risk for gender-based violence, harassment, abuse, and exploitation as remaining household members may not be decision-makers or responsible for households needs."

So your wife and daughter might be living in a house with a bunch of strange men and that may or may not end well. And that is not the only way your lifestyle will be impacted: "Community celebrations (religious holidays), bereavement (funerals) and other rites of passage are cornerstones of many societies. Proactive planning ahead of time, including strong community engagement and risk communication is needed to better understand the issues and concerns of restricting individuals from participating in communal practices because they are being shielded. Failure to do so could lead to both interpersonal and communal violence."

It is clear the creators of the shielding approach have a full awareness of the severity of what they are devising as they anticipate violence. They are vague in their description of what personnel will be assigned to oversee these green zones and in what capacity, but the subtext necessitates armed oversight. Something like this is not achievable any other way. Either they are planning to have done away with the 2nd amendment (there's that pesky Constitution again) or they will have to strip each "HH" of any weapons.

An operation like this would take some organization. Luckily the Rural Domestic Preparedness Consortium has been offering classes, in particular, MGT-433: Isolation and Quarantine for Rural Communities: A Whole Community Approach. They describe their course as: "This 8.0-hour, instructor-led course is designed to provide the knowledge necessary to begin planning for situations requiring the isolation and quarantine (I&Q) of a large portion of a local, rural population."

I suppose rural areas will be a bit harder to manage. It's easier to fence in a neighborhood than 3 farmhouses separated by 5 square miles of fields in the middle of nowhere. Don't think they haven't thought about it.

COVID-19 established a precedent for installing all manner of anti-human globalist policies to inch us ever closer to their New World Order, but it does not itself constitute the entirety of the attack on free civilization. There are other items being considered by people like Klaus Schwab who acknowledges that a massive cyber attack would offer a better opportunity for a Great Reset than even COVID-19 did.

Kopf

Cyber Polygon

Cyber Polygon is an annual international online training convened in 2020 to combat cyber attacks. It happened to arrive in a timely fashion as events such as pipeline and meat processing shutdowns (both globalist areas of interest) due to "cyber attacks" began occurring just around the time it arose. Klaus Schwab has warned us that a cyber attack will be coming that will make the COVID-19 pandemic pale in comparison, just as we had been assured that a pandemic would be coming right before it did.

A Cyber Polygon meeting was scheduled for July 8, 2022 but was later cancelled. Coincidentally, July 8, 2022 is the date that many ATM's and internet banking were shut down throughout Canada. Though this was not attributed to a cyber attack, it functioned just like one and offered the Polygon group a convenient opportunity to observe the social response to this related phenomenon that was so curiously timed.

The 2020 Cyber Polygon report begins with comments from some influential members, including one from Klaus Schwab: "One of the most striking transformations caused by the pandemic has been our transition to the digital 'everything' (p. 4)."

The following pages reflect Schwab's sentiments, stating that, "The 2020 pandemic has further accelerated digital transformation… the global digital transformation is opening truly unlimited opportunities for humanity…".

Well thank God for the pandemic. It has really been a blessing in so many ways. The threat identified by the WEF and Cyber Polygon team is that cybercriminals are on the rise which means increased data theft. "A single data breach across the ocean could trigger a chain reaction and spark a digital pandemic across the globe (p. 9)."

The 2020 training attracted 120 of the largest Russian and international organizations from 29 countries. These included banks, telecom companies, energy suppliers, healthcare institutions, universities as well as state and law enforcement agencies. The participants were the Blue Team and were tasked with protecting their segments of the training infrastructure while the organizers were the Red Team which simulated the cyber attacks on the Blue Team.

What they concluded is that the global community must unite in its efforts to prevent large scale cyber attacks. Of course only a globalist resolution could suffice. The people behind Cyber Polygon tend to make statements that make it appear as though global digitalization was one of their primary aims that COVID-19 just fortuitously assisted them in being able to achieve. Here's one from Herman Gref, CEO, Chairman of the Executive Board, Sberbank on page 20: "COVID-19 has accelerated various processes. Before the pandemic, we had been rather critical of digitalization because of all the problems brought about by the new technologies. Now, everybody is beginning to understand that this process is inevitable, we need to move forward and cybersecurity plays a great role in tech innovation."

On page 21, Sebastian Tolstoy states, "5G will be the platform for the society, for hospitals, for public transport, for everything that is to be connected. You need to have absolute trust in the underlying infrastructure, hence there is a high demand for security. Today we cannot even imagine what capabilities the new 5G network will enable, and artificial intelligence will obviously be one of the key features of our technologies and tools in the development of new application services. AI can be used for predictive analytics to improve performance, maintenance, and security of the network."

This is followed by a plug for digital identification on page 22: "A digital identity can become one of the effective ways of communication between the state and individual citizens."

Anyone that has spent any time thinking about some of the pitfalls of digital identification likely understands the extent to which it would enable an authoritarian government to strip personal liberties bare. Again, we see this push toward the decimation of human freedoms as is characteristic of these NWO documents. And again, the authors are fully aware that there will be resistance, and therefore promote the silencing of their voices: "In the era of digitalization, fake news has become a dangerous weapon being used by cybercriminals to attack people and organizations."

The "fake news" sources they're referencing are the only ones that will warn people about the dangers of digital identification. The globalists obviously have an awareness of what the citizenry is capable of in terms of technological innovation as evidenced by the "hack attack" scenario in the 2010 Rockefeller document. They know that typically, private citizens innovate, and governments then commandeer the technology. Since technology that is not controlled by the government is a threat to their power structure, they seek to impose regulations to preserve it any way they can. Anybody would be happy to never have to deal with identity theft online ever again, but the true role of Cyber Polygon seems to be to develop safeguards not *for* the people, but to protect their upcoming digital domination *from* the people.

They know that complete control of the cyber world is necessary in a technocracy. Their plans for a digital ID could not be effectively carried forth if citizen hackers can just unravel all their progress. Why would they do that? Because it will become abundantly clear that the digital ID is a slave system once they attach a social credit score to it, which of course would be the intent. They've said so. In a social credit system, if you say the wrong thing, you'll be penalized. If you exceed your carbon allotment, you'll be penalized. You will do as you're told or your funds will disappear and you won't eat.

One front being used to promote this agenda is vaccine passports which we were told was a conspiracy theory.

Kopf

Digital Documentation of COVID-19 Certificates: Vaccination Status

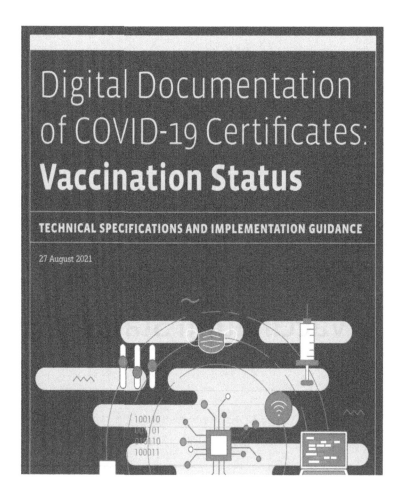

Digital Documentation of COVID-19 Certificates: Vaccination Status, which will be abbreviated as DDCC:VS, was published by the World Health Organization in August of 2021. It establishes a digital tracking framework for COVID-19 vaccinations to be adopted by member states of the WHO and funneled into a global database. It describes a system for digital identification, a process for verifying a private citizen's vaccination status, and snapshots of what it will look like.

From the very beginning in the executive summary, the WHO acknowledges that this isn't really about healthcare at all: "A digital vaccination certificate that documents a person's current vaccination status to protect against COVID-19 can then be used for continuity of care or as proof of vaccination for purposes other than health care."

Purposes other than health care. This is reiterated later on page xiv: "Vaccination records can also provide proof of vaccination status for purposes not related to health care." In this regard, the digital vaccine ID can be better understood as a permission slip for whether one is allowed to work, go to a grocery store, see a loved one at the hospital, or participate in society at all.

The beginning of Section 3 states, "In the context of COVID-19, the use of a vaccination record for Continuity of Care is primarily to: ensure that individuals know if, and when, they will need a subsequent dose; for health workers to use the proof of COVID-19 vaccination to decide on provision of health services based on medical history."

In other words, this system will help corrupt medical providers decide whether or not they want you to be alive. If you're a good statist and have received your vaccination as commanded, you may live, if not, you die. This may sound like an over-exaggeration on my part, but it isn't. There have already been multiple cases where people, even children, have been denied life-saving care due to not being vaccinated with a substance that the CDC has now openly acknowledged is killing people.

This is intended to be a global system as stated on page 18: "The HCID SHALL be used to establish a globally unique identifier (ID) for the DDCC:VS."

Page 52: "There should be clear and transparent processes for revocation of a DDCC:VS in case fraud has occurred, incorrect information needs to be rectified, faulty vaccine batches have been discovered or issues have been detected within the vaccine supply chain... Individuals will need to be informed if their DDCC:VS has been revoked and for what reason. Enforcing revocation without clearly communicated justification may lead to erosion of trust in governing bodies."

In other words, let's not forget we are trying to appear trustworthy. In addition to that, they actually acknowledge there could possibly be a faulty vaccine batch. That kind of rhetoric is considered misinformation on social media.

This document is about 80 pages long but it is filled with a good deal of technical information that entails the specifications and guidance for implementing their system as a general outline that member states can adopt and enhance, so there is little more to be said about it. The important thing to note is that globalists are spending a lot of time, effort, and money on developing a system for digital identification and insinuating that it is not intended to be limited to the health care arena. It is intended that individual nations use their own version of digital identification as long as that data is ultimately provided to the WHO for their global tracking database.

Food Chain Reaction – A Global Food Security Game

This food security game, conducted in November 2015 and published in December 2015, entails a hypothetical scenario spanning from 2020-2030 (chronologically consistent with Agenda 2030) "to better understand the global impacts of and responses to deepening global food system disruptions."

The scenario begins in 2020 and 2021 when food prices begin climbing. From 2022-2024 oil/gas prices rise dramatically and the grain supply from Russia and Ukraine are reduced. On page v the game design is introduced: "Food Chain Reaction—A Global Food Security Game was held November 9–10, 2015 in Washington, DC. Players with considerable influence and deep expertise in agriculture, trade and economics, climate and the environment, diplomacy, and security represented national and international governing bodies and organizations and the private sector. During the game, players encountered a decade marked by food price and supply swings amidst burgeoning population growth, rapid urbanization, severe weather events, and social unrest."

There are those bogeymen that typify NWO documents – climate change and population growth. Luckily the teams found that these issues could be solved with globalism: "Teams deepened their commitment to global and regional cooperation and collaboration during crisis periods, in large part due to players' open acknowledgement that no one nation, organization, or business could adequately address global food security (p. vii)."

Page 12: "The final round of play culminated in the convening of a Global Summit on Climate Security and Vulnerability during which representatives of all teams, except the Business and Investors team, which was not invited, expressed the desire for a more robust global coordination mechanism, with greater capacity to respond to climate-related conflict and food system volatility."

The scenario begins on page 25 of the report: "We begin the decade in 2020 with a growing global economy and oil prices at $75 a barrel. Food stocks are tighter than average. Global food commodity prices—while below the record highs of nearly a decade ago—remain at nearly 1.5 times long-term averages. Food prices in 2020 and 2021 are climbing, the result of weather-related disruptions to agricultural production."

"Things turn worse in 2023... China and India experience drought. Chinese scientists report that declines in underground water are disrupting irrigation, exacerbated by policies focused on achieving self-sufficiency in rice and wheat. Heat and dryness in India damage crop yields, cause heat stroke in the population, and affect power production. Russia and Ukraine experience heat stress that reduces grain supplies. By the end of 2023, tight global stocks push food prices upward even further, beyond the 2007–2012 peaks of 280 percent. The impacts register in many dimensions. Urban poor in the most vulnerable geographies become increasingly food insecure. Relief agencies issue urgent pleas for contributions. Organization of Petroleum Exporting Countries (OPEC) members, prompted by food import budget stress, organize strict production controls driving petroleum above $100 per barrel. Despite United States and European Union actions to reduce biofuels mandates, biofuels production remains steady, continuing to aggravate the food balance (p. 28)."

Though the specifics of the above paragraph may not reflect reality, many of the challenges that we are now facing in the present (January 2023 at the time of this writing) are accurately reflected; trouble with Russia and Ukraine, minimal crop yields, and the cost of oil, for example.

And surprise, surprise, the solution is to give power to the United Nations: "Although the parties involved in the summit did not finalize an agreement, they did concur on the general framework for a near-future agreement. Key initiatives in the framework included:

• Strengthening existing institutions and authorities under the United Nations (e.g., the World Food Programme, the World Health Organization, the Food and Agriculture Organization, the Department of Peacekeeping Operations, the Office of the High Commissioner for Refugees, and the International Fund for Agricultural Development) and developing better coordination among them.

• Establishing a new coordinating entity under the United Nations/G20 to create the capacity to respond in a more timely way (p. 15)."

Also, "Generous donations to the World Food Programme in 2024–2025, combined with lower food prices, leave the world well prepared to handle the catastrophe in areas humanitarian groups can reach. Also, measures such as the U.S. carbon tax and India's coal tax put climate change higher on the global agenda in the aftermath of the mid-decade price spike, leading to renewed attention (p. 31)."

Well look at that, carbon taxes and globalism save the world! The COP27 roundtable held on November 7th, 2022 yielded the same conclusion. They spoke out of both sides of their mouths, stating that there was a need to "shift to resilient agriculture, reduce losses in food production chain including through cooling solutions," and then go on to say that "food systems are also a major contributor to GHG emissions (about 1/3 of global emissions)."

Such cooling solutions involve the spraying of particulates into the stratosphere (called stratospheric aerosol injection) to block the sun's life-giving rays. This climate alarmism is also responsible for equally idiotic solutions like forcing Dutch farmers to reduce their farms by 1/3.

COP27 also identifies humanity itself as a problem: "Global food demand continues to grow as the world's population is expected to hit the mark of 9.6 bn by 2050. Meanwhile, 820m people are suffering from hunger as of 2021." If only there weren't so many people alive, there would be less hunger! I can't dispute the logic. Dead people can't be hungry.

The Rockefeller's Reset the Table plan identifies the overuse of water as a problem as well. Perhaps it is, but the solutions that people like this develop just contribute more to the problem. For example, you may recall that during California's drought in 2022, the government ordered water to be pumped into the ocean to help the fish rather than given to rice farmers. As a result, thousands upon thousands of acres of rice were not produced. Another of those "in harmony with nature" solutions.

According to the Rockefeller Foundation, "the pandemic has highlighted some of the promising solutions around the country and inspired new innovations (page 6 of Reset the Table, which was published in July of 2020, about the same time Schwab's Great Reset book was published)." Those new innovations emerged awfully fast. Almost like they were already made, just waiting for the right opportunity to be introduced.

The biggest takeaway from the Rockefeller Foundation's Reset the Table plan is their number one directive to "relentlessly apply true cost accounting" which means factoring in how much the production of an item harms the environment. It's calling for a carbon tax. The argument is that agriculture harms the environment, but this can be remedied by increasing the cost of agricultural products: "Private sector companies can incorporate true cost accounting practices as a better way to demonstrate to shareholders and stakeholders the company's sustainable business growth. French multinational food and beverage company Danone, for example, now reports a carbon-adjusted earnings per share."

They quietly acknowledge this will not be efficient: "While in some cases direct costs associated with the food system might go up, health care costs and the externalized costs of climate and environmental harms should come down." *Should* come down. They won't. Namely because the environmental harms don't exist.

The "solutions" that globalists develop just make matters worse – pump water into the ocean, spray the sky with reflective particulates, shut down agriculture and make fake meat – and the recommendations of Cargill's Food Security Game of 2015 to give more power to the UN will result in more of the same kinds of "solutions". These are the people behind the food scarcity in the first place.

Our homes, our energy, our water, our food, and our freedom are all under attack by an anti-human force. The ultimate agenda is one of transhumanism. People like Klaus Schwab, Yuval Noah Harari, and Ray Kurzweil all speak of a technocratic utopia, wherein a contingent of scientific elite, having achieved a technological apotheosis (that is, achieved godhood via AI technology), will rule over the serfs (us). They speak of something called the Internet of Bodies, in which humans are filled with nanotechnology that constantly surveils them from the inside out. Not only is your speech monitored, but your thoughts are monitored and your behaviors are controlled. Their ideal is that free will be a thing of the past as Harari has stated.

Transhumanism will be central to their New World Religion. Once the majority of humanity dies off per their depopulation protocol, the remainder will be isolated in 15-minute smart cities and relentlessly monitored while the elites seek to transform what it means to be human as they have openly stated.

Exploring Biodigital Convergence

From Policy Horizons Canada, copyrighted in 2019 under Her Majesty, The Queen, Exploring Biodigital Convergence is a document that does just that – explores biodigital convergence. Biodigital convergence is what it sounds like – the melding of organic life with machines.

This is not specific to Canada. Prime Minister Justin Trudeau is openly a World Economic Forum actor and Klaus Schwab has stated that the WEF essentially controls the Canadian government. There is reason to believe he is correct. COVID-19, mandatory vaccines, digital currency, orchestrated famine, and global cyber crashes are just antecedent events to destroy the world so they can "build it back better", and "better" to them means "a post-human era" which is driven by Atheistic Darwinian evolution that transcends natural biology.

The document begins with a foreword written by the Director General of Policy Horizons Canada, Kristel Van der Elst who writes, "Biological and digital systems are converging, and could change the way we work, live, and even evolve as a species" and it "may transform the way we understand ourselves and cause us to redefine what we consider human or natural."

The summary on page 6 defines biodigital convergence: "Digital technologies and biological systems are beginning to combine and merge in ways that could be profoundly disruptive to our assumptions about society, the economy, and our bodies. We call this the biodigital convergence." It goes on to say that this convergence is "opening up strikingly new ways to: change human beings – our bodies, minds and behaviors, change or create other organisms, and alter ecosystems." Yes, they want change human minds/behaviors, make new creatures, and terraform the world. A science fiction alien takeover plot would hardly be any different.

Page 9 begins an explanation of the distinction between 3 different ways in which biodigital convergence is occurring:

1) Full physical integration of biological and digital entities. This involves "the physical meshing, manipulating, and merging of the biological and digital creating new forms of life." It is also stated that, "New human bodies and new senses of identity could arise as the convergence continues."

2) Coevolution of biological and digital technologies. "For example, gene sequencing combined with AI leads to understanding genetic expression, which is then used to alter existing organisms to create organic compounds in new ways or even entirely new synthetic organisms... There is also a blurring between what is considered natural or organic and what is digital, engineered, or synthetic."

3) Conceptual convergence of biological and digital systems. "We could see a shift away from vitalism – the idea that living and nonliving organisms are fundamentally different because they are thought to be governed by different principles. Instead, the idea of biology as having predictable and digitally manageable characteristics may become increasingly common as a result of living in a biodigital age."

Humans are hackable animals.
-Yuval Noah Harari

The document further speculates via fictionalized narratives in the same fashion as the 2010 Rockefeller document and others. The first of these begins on page 16: "I wake up to the sunlight and salty coastal air of the Adriatic Sea. I don't live anywhere near the Mediterranean, but my AI, which is also my health advisor, has prescribed a specific air quality, scent, and solar intensity to manage my energy levels... My AI recommends a 'forest day'. I think 'okay' and my AI and neural implant do the rest... Building codes and home energy infrastructure are synchronized and require all homes be autoregulated for efficiency... I check my carbon offset measure to see how much credit I will receive for my home's contribution to the government's climate change mitigation program... While I'm brushing my teeth, Jamie, my personal AI, asks if I'd like a delivery drone to come pick up my daughter's baby tooth, which fell out two days ago. The epigenetic markers in children's teeth have to be analyzed and catalogued on our family genetic blockchain in order to qualify for the open health rebate... I'll admit it sounds gross, but it's a good thing the municipality samples our fecal matter from the sewage pipes. It's part of the platform to analyze data on nutritional diversity... The buildings in my neighborhood share a vertical farm, so I get carbon credits by eating miso made from soybeans produced on my roof and fermented by my fridge... As my coffee pours I check my daughter's latest school project, which has been growing on the counter for the past week. She's growing a liver for a local puppy in need as part of her empathy initiative at school. More stem cells are on the way to start a kidney too because she wants to help more animals. I grab my coffee, brewed with a new certified carbon-negative bean variety, and sit on the couch for a minute... First I get the debrief from colleagues finishing their work day on the other side of the world. I shiver momentarily as I think about how intimately we're all connected in this digital biosphere – then it passes" – a reference to the IoB, or Internet of Bodies. This segment concludes with an acknowledgement that the story may sound far-fetched, but that the technology to make it happen currently exists.

There is a table beginning on page 22 that offers "new ways to change human beings... monitoring, altering, and manipulating human thoughts and behaviors." Let me say that again: monitoring, altering, and manipulating human thoughts. Altering and manipulating human thoughts. It also offers new ways to "monitor, manage, and influence bodily functions, as well as predict, diagnose, and treat disease." This is especially exciting as that means they can predict an impending health crisis (likely created by them whether real or imagined) and just get you "vaccinated" with nanobots preemptively. They also note that there already exists a patent that will allow Alexa to detect a cough or cold.

On page 24 it goes on to say that "nanobots and nanomaterials can operate and precisely deliver drugs within living creatures." Perhaps this means that the nanotechnology discovered within COVID-19 vaccines by scientists in New Zealand, Spain, and elsewhere are currently holding drugs to be released at whatever point their programming dictates. These kinds of things will become more common as the text states, "artificial intelligence can help design microorganisms with specific characteristics."

No technocratic takeover would be complete without terraforming. The text states on page 27 that biodigital convergence will create new ways to alter ecosystems, including "changing and eradicating entire species". They mean this of course for malaria-spreading mosquitoes and things like that. We hope. They'd also like to be "altering the natural environment at scale... geoengineering approaches that accurately model carbon capture of solar reflectance," while noting that it is already possible today to engineer microorganisms in peatland to store and capture carbon and offset climate change.

They mention 23andme on page 32 as an example of noteworthy genetic ingenuity and praise lab meat as globalists tend to: "This includes the ability to create food and engineer meat without the need for arable land. Lab-grown meat – cells that develop to produce muscle cells and cultured meat in a monitored environment -- could be a game-changer in decentralizing multiple industries from farming to shipping."

Perhaps that is why Bill Gates in buying up vast swaths of farmland while investing in these synthetic foods. After all, the document states, "Industrial districts may rise in value at the expense of agricultural land".

And what globalist agenda would be complete without advocating for bug-consumption as they do in this scenario of a hypothetical company offered on page 39: "90% of the animal protein is sustainably sourced from specially engineered insects. The catch? You have to grant the company access and data rights to your entire biome to receive the product and its purported health benefits."

On page 34 the authors admit, "the technologies and applications featuring biodigital convergence will not be able to operate without a lot of data... Bioprospecting is already an important aspect of drug development and may rise in importance – and provoke greater controversy in healthcare. The full potential of biodigital convergence may therefore require a constant flow of data... The data-reliant nature of biodigital convergence means that the demand for data could increase substantially – particularly human, animal, plant, and bacterial data. Large platforms could potentially gather and control large amounts of information about individuals, their context, and the natural world."

On page 39, the authors lay out a potential hazard in the following hypothetical scenario: "A leading Canadian supermarket is having a bad year. It's been embroiled in a scandal over several features of its loyalty program. The "Your Choice" program offers special discounts and preemptive ordering if you allow it full access to your digital twin – essentially giving it full access to your life and activity. A leaked internal report suggests that this data is being used in conjunction with intrusive neurotechnologies to encourage members to consume more. At the centre of the scandal is the fact that the supermarket is essentially selling access to the minds of 'Your Choice' members". They go on to state, "The relationship between firms and individuals may require higher levels of trust, as firms seek access to highly intimate data about our lives and bodies." They also note the possibility of synthetic biology leading to military applications, stating that "microorganisms can produce disease-causing agents or toxins" and that there is also "the potential for malicious, reckless, or accidental release of deadly lab-made viruses", which is exactly what happened just following this publication.

On page 42 in the governance section the authors state that "there is an important distinction between what is technologically possible and what is socially acceptable".

Note that their concern is for what is socially acceptable, not what is morally acceptable, i.e., "how much can we get away with before people revolt". They wrap it up on page 43 by insinuating that increasing people's lifespans using this technology may not be the best idea because it could "challenge tax, social security, and health care" and we could see a negative impact in retirement funds, public healthcare expenses, and elderly accommodation. This subtle endorsement for having fewer humans on planet earth concludes the document.

Kopf

Global Governance

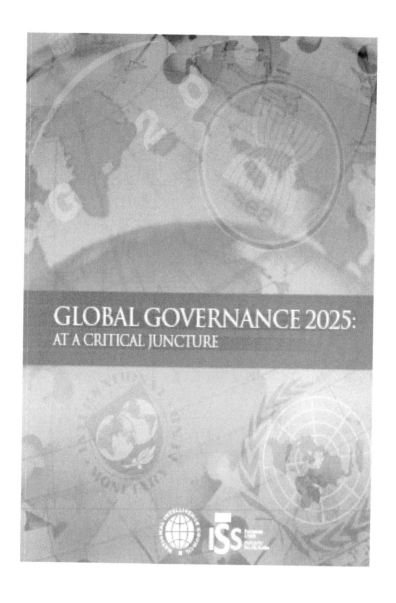

GLOBAL GOVERNANCE 2025:
AT A CRITICAL JUNCTURE

Global Governance 2025 is a report completed by the National Intelligence Council and the European Union Institute for Security Studies in September of 2010. It defines global governance as "the collective management of common problems at the international level" and claims that the world is at a critical juncture as emerging threats are now harder to contain due to rapid globalization. The report offers four hypothetical scenarios to explore how best to govern the world.

"Throughout the main text, we have sprinkled fictionalized scenarios that could result if, as we believe likely, the multiple and diverse governance frameworks struggle to keep pace with the looming number of transnational and global challenges. The scenarios illustrate various permutations that could happen over the next 15 years. The following summarizes what we see as the principal potential trajectories of the international system as it tries to confront new challenges. We believe the risks of an unreformed global governance system are likely to accumulate over time. Crises—so long as they are not overwhelming—may actually spur greater innovation and change in the system. Inaction over the long term increases the risks of a complete breakdown."

"**Scenario I: Barely Keeping Afloat.** In this scenario, seen as the most likely one over the next several years, no one crisis will be so overwhelming as to threaten the international system even though collective management advances slowly. Crises are dealt with ad hoc and temporary frameworks or institutions are devised to avert the most threatening aspects of them. Formal institutions remain largely unreformed and Western states probably must shoulder a disproportionate share of "global governance" as developing countries prevent disruptions at home. This future is not sustainable over the longer term as it depends on no crisis being so unmanageable as to overwhelm the international system."

"**Scenario II: Fragmentation**. Powerful states and regions try to wall themselves off from outside threats. Asia builds a regional order that is economically self-sufficient. Global communications ensure globalization does not die, but it slows significantly. Europe turns its focus inward as it wrestles with growing discontent with declining living standards. With a growing work force, the US might be in a better position but may still be fiscally constrained if its budgetary shortfalls and long-term debt problems remain unresolved."

"**Scenario III: Concert of Europe Redux**. Under this scenario, severe threats to the international system—possibly a looming environmental disaster or a conflict that risks spreading—prompt greater cooperation on solving global problems. Significant reform of the international system becomes possible. Although less likely than the first two scenarios in the immediate future, such a scenario might prove the best outcome over the longer term, building a resilient international system that would step up the level of overall cooperation on an array of problems. The US increasingly shares power while China and India increase their burden sharing and the EU takes on a bigger global role. A stable concert could also occur incrementally over a long period in which economic gaps shrink and per capita income converges."

"**Scenario IV: Gaming Reality: Conflict Trumps Cooperation**. This scenario is among the least likely, but the possibility cannot be dismissed. The international system becomes threatening owing to domestic disruptions, particularly in emerging powers such as China. Nationalistic pressures build as middle-class aspirations for the "good life" are stymied. Tensions build between the United States and China, but also among some of the BRICs as competition grows for secure resources and clients. A nuclear arms race in the Middle East could deal an equally destabilizing blow to prospects for continued global growth. Suspicions and tensions make reforming global institutions impossible; budding regional efforts, particularly in Asia, also are undermined."

Not much detail is offered in the way of the fictionalized events, however, the document focuses more on discussions surrounding each hypothetical situation. The text seems to indicate that the global governors are engaged in large scale experimentation: "Innovative approaches to global governance are developed through trial and error. Some of these experiments will not stand the test of time, but on the whole they expose a fundamental trend toward looser, more flexible, ad hoc and sometimes more accountable forms of cooperation (p. 18)."

Never missing an opportunity to point out the benefits of catastrophe, the authors write, "A crisis such as an environmental catastrophe or the implosion of a large failed state could spark cooperation, but a reactive approach to such extreme contingencies probably would prove inadequate (p. 18-19)."

After offering some praise for the great contributions of the Bill and Melinda Gates Foundation on page 25, a concern is raised: "Maybe we are seeing a shift that is not geographical but horizontal—we are seeing the emergence of a global management elite and wondering what that means for the future of liberal democracy."

Page 37 offers a fictionalized account taking place the summer of 2021: "In summer 2021, I—admittedly a bored diplomat—find myself sequestered for several weeks in Perth (Australia). A new outbreak of bird flu, despite the rapid quarantines put in place, has spread and closed down most major airports. I am trying to get back to Europe for my annual leave, but most connections have been cut. To while away the time, I am thinking back on world events. The current international scene holds an uncanny resemblance to a computer game called "Peace Hero" I used to play with my son years ago. Unlike most games, this one was constructed so you earned points for finding ways to cooperate with fellow contestants, all of whom assumed roles of major countries or international organizations. The world was confronted, for example, with a pandemic— not unlike the present—and the challenge was to find which countries could provide emergency vaccines. The game actually prompted you to construct a UN Security Council resolution that would quickly be voted into action. The game was probably never a best seller, but it had intrigued me, particularly how the players perverted its intended objective."

Again, it seems as though globalists have been daydreaming for many years about all the benefits that pandemics might someday bring, even projecting their possible date of occurrence to be approximate to the time that COVID-19 did in fact occur. The solution tends to always be the same: call on the UN for salvation.

Conclusion

The documents included in this book certainly do not represent the totality of all the writings of the proselytes of the New World Order, though I believe that when considered in conjunction with one another, they sufficiently demonstrate a premeditated globalist plan to centralize power by means of a pandemic orchestrated by the likes of those who attend secret meetings in Davos and engage in strange rituals at the Bohemian Grove. That such meetings and rituals take place is no longer disputed as both have been factually and officially established.

Some documents were omitted from the book such as the National Strategy for Countering Domestic Terrorism, which, though useful in demonstrating the targeting of people with anti-globalist sentiments by the United States government, did not entirely correspond with the overall theme of the book, save for the implicit tyranny throughout. I invite the reader to visit NWOdocuments.com to review documents such as that and others that were not included here. The documents contained in this book can also be located at the website for closer review. My intent is to provide tangible evidence of my claims that can be verified. The quotations are verbatim and the page numbers are included so that they can be located and confirmed.

For the last few months, I have been sending out newsletters to those who subscribe to the website. These contain a smattering of current events, thoughts on making preparations, and other miscellaneous discourse. It occurred to me that it may be of some benefit to include a glimpse into the real-life fallout of these documents as relevant events continue to occur, and being that I am not one to reinvent the wheel, figured it may be easiest to simply include the newsletters here. Maybe someday down the road it will be interesting to look back on.

Appendix

Newsletter 1 – The Guidestones Have Fallen

July 8, 2022

Greetings,

You have likely heard by now that the Georgia Guidestones have been destroyed. Video footage reveals a strong explosion shattering one of the pillars of the occult monument and damaging the capstone. Some have hypothesized that this was due to a lightning strike, but the media reports that this was an intentional demolition as there were additional explosive devices left behind that did not ignite. At any rate, the guidestones no longer stand in Georgia as the remaining structure was toppled due to safety concerns. Good riddance. But let's not forget the anti-human tenets of this detestable monument:

1. Maintain humanity under 500,000,000 in perpetual balance with nature.
2. Guide reproduction wisely – improving fitness and diversity.
3. Unite humanity with a living new language.
4. Rule passion – faith – tradition – and all things with tempered reason.
5. Protect people and nations with fair laws and just courts.
6. Let all nations rule internally resolving external disputes in a world court.
7. Avoid petty laws and useless officials.
8. Balance personal rights with social duties.
9. Prize truth – beauty – love – seeking harmony with the infinite.
10. Be not a cancer on the Earth – Leave room for nature – Leave room for nature.

Looking at these through the iconic "They Live" sunglasses, you might see something like:

1. Massive genocidal depopulation
2. Eugenics and transhumanism
3. Rebuild the Tower of Babel
4. Eradicate religion and morality
5. Fair and just by liberal globalist standards, like the January 6 show trials
6. Double speak: nations have autonomy but world government reigns supreme
7. Useless officials like those who advocate for national sovereignty
8. Subtly disregard personal freedoms in favor of creating slaves to the state
9. "Truth, beauty, and love" as defined by people who believe Lucifer is the bearer of light and truth
10. Full circle reiteration of the depopulation agenda, regarding humanity as a disease

As we have seen, the green movement seems only to be a euphemism for human extinction. These druidic nature worshipers constantly prattle on about how glorious the eradication of humans (not themselves though) would be for the planet. Such a statement – which is unfortunately not uncommon to hear at present – is necessarily arrogant beyond comprehension as the individuals holding this view never mean for themselves to be eradicated. No, they are good. It's all the other people that deserve to die. This is evidenced by the fact that they never seem to kill themselves though they maintain that the fewer humans, the better.

I have heard speculation that perhaps it was the elites themselves that demolished their own monument as a form of ritual destruction, to create order from chaos as they would put it. I've heard it said that the destruction of the guidestones is not a good thing as evidence for their existence can now be better obscured. I've also heard some fair skepticism about why the mainstream media is bringing any attention to this at all as this seems to be a thing that they'd historically selectively omit in an effort to steer attention away from their secretive overlords.

Many secrets remain concerning the ominous guidestones. I would be interested to hear your thoughts on the subject. If you have any insights to share, feel free to utilize the forum on NWOdocuments.com so that we can interact as a community, which is what the NWO is working overtime to ensure does not happen.

My intention is to continue sending out newsletters. If you know someone who might enjoy receiving them, feel free to share the website with them and encourage them to subscribe. Free speech on social media may soon become a thing of the past. We know the Johns Hopkins Center for Health Security and others are working hard at ensuring this. You may think that just sharing a simple post, document, or article changes nothing, but if that was the case, they wouldn't try so hard to ensure it doesn't happen.

Let's stay in touch and continue working together to shed light on the lies of the globalist agenda.

Newsletter 2 – Unusual July

July 15, 2022

Very soon after I had posted the invitation to this website/newsletter on Tik Tok they banned me. My new profile is simply "nwodocuments" for a few weeks until the next inevitable ban. Attempts at creating another backup profile have been thus far unsuccessful as I am just redirected to my current profile. But again, this newsletter will serve as my means of informing you of my next profile when I am forced to create a new account entirely.

July 2022 has gotten off to an interesting start. In less than a week, the following (and much more) occurred:

July 4: Dutch farmers revolt against government mandated food demolition
July 5: Large hadron collider at CERN resumes after being shut down since 2018
July 6: The Georgia Guidestones are bombed
July 7: Prime Minister of the UK resigns
July 8: Former Prime Minister of Japan is assassinated
July 8: Cyber attack in Canada coinciding with scheduled Cyber Polygon meeting
July 8: Elon Musk withdraws from Twitter deal
July 9: President of Sri Lanka announces resignation

Just before all that on June 30 there were significant internet shutdowns across multiple providers in Sudan. These events, when considered with the WEF's promise that devastating cyber attacks are imminent, serve as our notification that they are gearing up for the crash they've guaranteed. I find it beyond coincidental that the internet and bank shutdowns in Canada occurred on the very date that the WEF/Interpol Cyber Polygon meeting was to take place. Of course, the official narrative is that the shutdown was not a cyber attack at all, yet it functioned exactly like one and just so happened to provide the Cyber Polygon clan a unique opportunity to observe the fallout of the very thing they obsess over on the very date they had scheduled their meeting.

Just before the shutdowns in Sudan, Roe versus Wade was overturned by the United States Supreme Court on June 24 after nearly 50 years. One wonders at the timing of it all. Why are so many seemingly unrelated and disparate events coming to a head simultaneously as if portending some greater impending disaster?

The list above is by no means exhaustive as there continue to be fuel and food plants exploding and burning down as well as uprisings against governments springing up in numerous nations across the globe. Though inspiring to see the spirit of the people revolting against tyranny, I can't help but remain trepidatious knowing that these uprisings are part of the Great Reset plan. As Klaus Schwab said, "We need to prepare for an angrier world". The vitriol of the people is no surprise to them. In fact, it's integral to their operation: 1) destroy nations with disruptive globalist policies implemented by bribed leaders, 2) wait for the people to overthrow their governments, 3) either use the disruption as justification to eliminate dissidents or exploit the opportunity to install a populist leader to save (further enslave) everyone, "penetrating the cabinets" as Mr. Schwab admitted on video is the tactic used by the WEF.

Meanwhile, professional athletes, well-known and lesser-known celebrities, and people we personally know continue to suffer significant health impairments or simply drop dead from "ill-defined and unknown causes of death" which have continued to rise following the vaccinations after having remained relatively steady in prior years. Major life insurance companies are warning of drastic increases in excess mortality that cannot be explained away by "long COVID". Even more alarming, many doctors and researchers are warning that most vaccine injuries have gone either unnoticed or unreported, and their manifestation is yet to come. I can personally attest to this, having witnessed significant injuries in others following vaccination that were attributed to another cause or no cause. Perhaps more alarming still is the fact that despite big pharma, big government, and big tech being fully aware that the current data now indicates that these vaccinations are not at all safe OR effective, they go on recklessly promoting them. Why? I can think of only two motives: money or malice.

Anecdotal data can be far more reliable than the bought-and-paid-for research propaganda of this day and age and it thoroughly defies the present narrative. I am consistently amazed at the sheer volume of commenters on social media that share their personal struggles following vaccination or the struggles of others in their lives who had been subjected to the poison. I recall a Facebook post from a local news agency that was soliciting stories of unvaccinated people who had died from COVID and what they received instead was a barrage of people sharing how they or their loved ones were injured or killed by the vaccine. Tens of thousands of them in fact. To not have predicted how that post would horribly backfire is a testament to how out-of-touch these narrative swallowers truly are.

Predictably, Elon Musk has withdrawn from the controversial Twitter deal. Of course, free speech being returned to the highly controlled mouthpiece of social engineering that is Big Tech, in this case Twitter, was only ever a fantasy. If freedom of speech was ever restored to social media (was it ever there in the first place?) the globalist agenda, which is only able to thrive on a gluttonous diet of rampant lies and deceit, would crumble. Tyranny cannot withstand freedom of speech, which is freedom of ideas; that is why it is one of the first things to be expunged by rising dictatorships. The ruling elite class would sooner blow up the entire world than let an entity as large and influential as Twitter allow its users to speak freely, which I don't believe Musk would have accomplished anyway. Not Musk, who is responsible for the global surveillance that Star Link enables. Musk, who is responsible for biodigital convergence via Neuralink. Musk, who even through Tesla is carrying forward the established goals of the The Great Reset. Musk, who procreates with Satanists. Musk, who speaks nationalist words to win over patriots and conservatives, and then goes on to achieve globalist aims that put Bill Gates to shame.

Should we be optimistic about the future of the world when humanity has collectively agreed to allow evil such a foothold through our indifference? Absolutely not. But we can be optimistic about our own individual futures. Just as not all of us endorsed evil while the rest of the world did, not all of us will be swept away as the rest of the world is. There are stories of soldiers in battle who survived terrible assaults – nothing left but rubble all around them though they remained untouched – because they knew they were up against an indestructible enemy, and without any real recourse to retaliate, they got on their knees and prayed, and lived.

Now is not the time to feign disbelief in God. There are no Atheists in foxholes. It is impossible for us to imagine our consciousness winking out of existence because it is impossible for such a thing to occur to something immutable like consciousness. Whether the wicked elite succeed in depopulating the planet or not, our demise is inevitable. We'll die someday either way. And when we do, we will certainly go somewhere. It is good to be on the right side of history but immeasurably better to be on the right side of eternity.

Newsletter 3 – Fearmonger

July 28. 2022

Those inclined to trade awareness for comfort often maintain that the tumult of current events is little more than a repeating cycle. History repeats itself after all. Unhinged people have always fear-mongered about impending doom from time immemorial. Everything will be fine. These kinds of things have always happened.

But they haven't.

At no other time in recorded history have we seen global initiatives at the magnitude of those we see today. At no other time has technology been sufficient to usurp what it means to be human via DNA alteration supported by an . insane contingent of transhumanist technocratic elites. At no other time in history has there been such a widespread prevalence of surveillance, propaganda, and speech control – no, Nazi Germany doesn't even come close. Never has anyone alive seen such a grotesque display of international social engineering. Yet because of the propaganda element, many do not comprehend what they see, using inane rebuttals against what is clearly before their very eyes.

When something anomalous occurs, the familiar call of the denialist raises its oblivious voice: "that's not suspicious at all, those things have always happened!" I heard it when an unprecedented increase in the cost of oil was forecasted. I heard it in response to the multiple coronavirus drills that were executed just weeks before the great COVID-19 psychological operation. I heard it when food plants began closing due to unusual circumstances up to and including planes crashing into them. I heard it when governments began restricting farmers from receiving water or planting their crops. I heard it when trains hauling fertilizer began to derail and fuel plants began exploding. And I'm hearing it now when freezer components are failing in multiple stores simultaneously, resulting in the destruction of tens of thousands of tons of food. Add it to the list of destroyed rice, potatoes, wheat, swine, poultry, cattle, etc. "This has always happened! It's normal!" the denialists insist. Yet they can never produce the data to demonstrate that these events have always occurred on a regular basis.

The reason they never produce data to validate their argument that these fires, animal slaughters, and fuel disasters have always occurred at this rate is that there is none. There is no such available data because the rate at which events such as these are currently occurring is absolutely unprecedented. If that was not the case, surely they would have laid to rest all these "wild conspiracies" long ago by producing evidence to substantiate their claims. It would be very easy to do. But they haven't because they can't. And we continue to witness these disasters occur on a regular basis, so frequently it seems to have become normalized.

The United States continues to pump billions of dollars into Ukraine (fueling the conflict, not helping it) while cutting off its own resources and ushering in millions upon millions of illegal immigrants to exacerbate its economic frailty to the greatest extreme possible. The sheer scale at which this is occurring is as unprecedented as the food and fuel disasters. By all appearances, this is a multi-pronged controlled demolition.

An armed nation requires special attention. What are the despots to do when every other household contains a firearm, making their lustful desires such as forcefully "inoculating" the citizenry impossible? How to achieve maximum tyranny when a people is not defenseless and all attempts at disarmament have thus far failed? I can think of very few ways to achieve the dominance they seek without first decimating the armed population.

People viewing the world through a lens of normalcy bias seem to enjoy pretending things like engineered famine are the stuff of conspiracies. Well, they are. Unfortunately, conspiracies are real and more prevalent than these people would like to believe. We've seen it before. Engineered famines such as the Holodomor are unfortunate historical facts. Even if that was not the case, we can know for certain that minimizing the human population is a fantasy of the globalists because it is in their white papers. Documents such as the United Nations' World Population Plan of Action and the United States' NSSM-200 demonstrate a long-planned agenda to depopulate the world, yes, even hinting at intentionally starving entire nations to death. Imagine what they state more overtly in the documents that remain classified.

No, democide is not a novel concept. Governments destroying their own people is nothing new. Acknowledging that it has happened in other nations but could never happen in our own is merely fear-driven wishful thinking. Rome fell, as do all empires. Yet stating as much will elicit unwarranted vitriol from the fearful. It is they who decry the observant and aware as "fear mongers".

Today Paul Revere would be called a scare monger for telling people "The British are coming!" Jesus would be accused of selling fear by warning people that as the end draws near there will be wars and rumors of wars, the Euphrates river will dry up, and the third temple will be rebuilt (all of which are occurring now). Yet how much wiser it is to prepare for the worst while hoping for the best as opposed to denying that the worst is even a remote possibility because the thought of it is too frightening. Denial is cowardice. Awareness saves.

Still, we are told by the denialists that there is nothing to worry about. They claim that they've been through this before during the Y2K scare of 1999 and again when many people believed that the world would end in 2012. The glaring difference between those scenarios and our current situation is that those were purely speculative, not based on events that have truly occurred, whereas now we are actually seeing governments being overthrown, QR codes being required in order to be allowed the luxury of fuel, forced vaccination, and even the erecting of camps to hold people against their will. This is not fanciful speculation, this is happening.

What is occurring in the world today has never been seen at this magnitude. There has been engineered food scarcity, yes, but not globally coordinated at this scale. There have been isolated declarations of health crises that served as justification to inject unsuspecting common people with deadly poisons for the sake of cold experimentation, but not at a global level. Since Nimrod's Tower we have not come so close to global governance as we are now. Never in recorded history has there been a war on truth so profound that even leaders in government and medicine claim that men can give birth. This is a world-permeating psychological assault. Insanity and debauchery have been declared virtuous. Good is called evil, and evil is called good. No, this is nothing like Y2K. This is something else. It is insidious, it is global, and it is happening whether you like it or not. If you prepare and nothing comes of it, you're no worse off. If you do not prepare and the WEF achieves its aims, you will die a fool. The question of how to prepare can be difficult to answer as there are different ways this could play out, but I will do my best to answer that in the next newsletter.

Governments have declared war on their own people (see the National Strategy for Countering Domestic Terrorism) and the infrastructure for arresting freedom-loving dissenters has been established (see documentation from the Johns Hopkins

Center for Health Security), including the involvement of the FBI, CIA, NSA, and recruitment of local law enforcement. We live in the days of social media technocracy. Your every post and comment is logged into a database and flagged as problematic if not in alignment with the new government religion. Did you dare to disagree with our latest climate change pseudo-data? Did you fail to take up the latest fake social justice cause? Did you voice doubt about the motives of your leaders? Well then off to the camps with you.

The denialists will scoff at the notion of camps as well, however, it's not as if camps are any more a novel idea than planned famines. They're not only a part of history, but of current events. There are people dying in Chinese prison camps today. New camps have been commissioned recently in countries like Australia, the US, the UK, and others. The CDC has published their plans for camps called Green Zones in America. The elite are not dedicating so much time, effort, and funding into planning and building camps merely for the fun of it. They're for you and me.

You have a social credit score already, and if you're reading this, it's probably a poor one. As you may have noticed, posts that have been made years ago are still being flagged for hate speech, disinformation, or any such nonsense. You could immediately cease making any posts presenting evidence that contradicts those narratives sanctioned by our compromised and traitorous governments and it would likely still make no difference. You've already been designated as a follower or dissenter. The consequence of this designation will not manifest until we enter into the digital currency that will be tied to our social credit scores and restricted by the government if we wave the wrong flag, say the wrong thing, or even think the wrong thought as they claim. Exile is the best-case scenario for any who insist on proclaiming truth and freedom.

This credit score will also be tied to what the elites call the IoB, or Internet of Bodies, which is a reference to your very essence being monitored by internal nanotechnology at all times, including your excrement, partially to determine whether you have been compliant or have instead broken the rules and consumed more than your allotted rations, in which case of course your social credit score (money) will be reduced. Everything will have a carbon rating ascribed to it. Every article of clothing you wear requires some degree of carbon expenditure to produce. As does every food item you consume. Every vacation you take. Perhaps even everything you say. After all, to point out that the polar ice caps remain as hardy as ever is to spread misinformation that could in turn cause others to lose faith in carbon-rationing practices, thus resulting in larger carbon footprints. This is unacceptable and must be punished. For the greater good of course.

However, it is my suspicion that the IoB is not merely a means of total biological surveillance, but also of total biological control. It is beyond my purview to understand such things, but I can't help but speculate that once nanotechnology is pumping through our veins, it could be activated in ways we would not enjoy. Naturally the selling point is that nanobots could be sent to ailing areas of our bodies to make repairs as needed, perhaps even curing terminal diseases. People will embrace transhumanism not because of the abhorrent possibilities, but because of the lifesaving and even life-extending benefits that it will be sold with. It will tantalize that primordial desire for eternal life, which will be counterfeit but very tempting, and any who stand against it (Christians certainly will) will be cheered to the gallows. People will be so blinded by the potential benefits that they will ignore the obvious pitfalls, such as extraordinary pain being remotely activated at the will of our controllers. As the scriptures state, "men will seek death, but not find it."

The terrible possibilities afforded by advances in CRISPR gene-editing technology and biodigital convergence technologies such as that being developed by Neuralink is yet another mark against the argument that we have seen these portents of doom before and it's not at all different than the fear mongering of years past. Unfortunately, friends, it is extremely different than anything you or I have seen before. Perhaps the fully realized transhuman age is years away, but the infrastructure of tyranny that is necessary to pave the way for it will be horrifying enough, and it seems likely that widespread depopulation will be one of the precursors.

The traditional accusation lodged against those of us with an impulse to sound the alarm is that we are selling fear, that is, we are seeking to profit from the fear we instill in others – an accusation that falls flat with nothing to substantiate it. I'd like to know where all my fear money is. I barely promote the books I've written, and they aren't priced such that I would make any noteworthy monetary gains from them anyway, there are no membership fees here, and Tik Tok, the platform on which this accusation is most frequently lodged against me, is certainly not about to pay me! The same is true for most of the mainstream speakers of truth. Sure, they may profit from their survival gear or storable food sales (they have to make a living somehow), but they'd likely generate a good deal more income by going green and touting the latest Leftist narrative. That's why major companies like Netflix stay woke even though it has resulted in a significant drop in revenue as multitudes of subscribers reject them; in the long run they make even more money because they are subsidized by Black Rock and Vanguard for propagating the new globalist antihuman religion.

No, "fear porn" is not the most ideal way to generate income or gain popularity. It is also a dishonest moniker. The onus of fear rests solely on the individual receiving the information, not on those that share it. Imagine a villager cautioning a tourist that a lion has been spotted in the area, and the tourist being angry at the villager for making him afraid. Let's thank God we are not so dense.

Things are likely about to go from bad to worse. The writing is on the wall. Only those as foolish as the aforementioned tourist would claim that everything is normal, nothing unusual is going on, and we have seen this all before. We certainly have not. Though throughout history there have been prison camps and wars and engineered famine, no one alive has ever seen such things occur on a global scale, no not even during the world wars. No one alive has seen such a level of transnational medical tyranny or dystopian technocratic global elitism. No, this isn't like Y2K. No, this has not happened before. I suspect it is fear that drives this denial, yet having an awareness of our plight does not necessitate fear. Fear can drive preparation, and the more prepared people are, the less fearful they need to be. That is one functional aspect of fear. It can motivate.

And there is no more pertinent function of fear than this: the mandate to work out our salvation with fear and trembling. Fear God alone. That is the foremost preparatory obligation.

Newsletter 4 – Prepare

August 10, 2022

When speaking of the globalist threat, the question of what we can do to stop it inevitably arises. My opinion, which I hope is incorrect, is that we can do nothing. The disease of far-Left ideals has proliferated beyond recovery. Once evil is allowed an inch, it takes a mile. We said it's ok to kill babies *sometimes,* and now there are states trying pass legislation that allows for babies to be murdered even days after they're born. We tolerated the social engineering of sexuality and now we're declared bigots for believing it's inappropriate for children to place dollar bills in the G-strings of drag queens. We tolerated the insanity of pretending to be the opposite sex and now people are losing their jobs for saying that men can't have babies. We fed evil, and evil bit our hands because that is what evil does.

What does any of that have to do with the globalist agenda? Everything. Moral bankruptcy, which requires the forfeiture of truth, paves the way for psychological destruction. When the collective social mind is so scrambled that it insists men can give birth, the stage is set for subversive tyrants to pour forth their ridiculous propaganda into the empty minds now thoroughly primed to receive nonsense. Hence, the most educated people in the world know for certain that cow flatulence has been destroying the planet all along and boys are really girls if only they say so. We are in the midst of global psychological warfare. I contend that the WEF could not have carried forth their Great COVID-19 Plan had the minds of the people not first been sufficiently softened by chemicals, immorality, and modern bread and circus.

Many people don't notice how far gone we now are because the progression has been incremental and therefore difficult to definitively identify. We are the frog in the pot that has been brought slowly to boil. Advocating for white genocide somehow became a virtue. Asking a simple and obvious question about a given government narrative has somehow become an act of terrorism. Insanity has become normalized in progressive, small doses escaping the notice of the people.

Momentum is the destructive force behind a tsunami. The question is whether the tsunami of globalist social engineering has gained momentum sufficient to become unstoppable. Because it is socially unacceptable to say simply, "it's okay to be white" or "men can't have babies", I believe that the psychological programming is so extraordinary that yes, the tsunami has gained momentum sufficient to be unstoppable. The globalist agenda is fueled by perpetual lies and could only be defeated by widespread rejection of those lies, however, people who have fallen in love with their own deception will not likely turn back to the truth. They have given evil an inch and it has taken a mile such that it is now even a sin to interfere with child grooming in schools. And this new antimoral code has become internationally institutionalized, inducted into the social fabric of nations.

What do we do to stop this? Well, how does one respond to a tsunami? Stopping it to save the village is not possible. You don't stop a tsunami, you flee to higher ground. You prepare ahead of time. Those who do not are swept away.

It is difficult to know exactly how to prepare when it is uncertain how the future will play out. Will there be nuclear war? Will your local compromised law enforcement come knocking on your door to force you into a labor camp for posting a meme on social media? Will the power grid be knocked out? Will there be enough food to eat in a year? There are varying degrees of preparation that can be achieved based on which events actually transpire. In the event of a nuclear detonation, for example, little can be done at ground zero.

What is easier to prepare for than a nuclear holocaust is food, water, and energy shortages, which in my opinion, are inevitable. Depending on factors such as legality, availability, and whether you happen to be in a free nation, arming oneself may be a good idea. Even if no firearms are available, there are other options. A firearm may not always be the best option anyway in an area where they've been outlawed. They are loud. They draw attention. In terms of procuring food, a pellet gun for small game or a crossbow for large game may be a good option as they are effective, but quiet.

For most people it is not realistic to depend on hunting, fishing, and gardening for providing all necessary sustenance. Vegetables, for example, provide very few calories, though they are wonderful for supplying vitamins, minerals, and health benefits. The macronutrients (protein, fat, and carbohydrates) required by your body are better supplied by animals (protein and fat anyway), which provide greater caloric density as well. Rabbits and chickens can be raised with relative ease, do not require wide swaths of farmland, and are far more beneficial in terms of calorie production than gardening.

Unless it is a large enough operation, not even chickens, rabbits, and gardens may be enough to survive on. Things happen. Coyotes clean out entire chicken coops. Weather events destroy crops. Therein lies the wisdom of acquiring dried goods such as white rice or lentils to store long-term. The drier, the longer the shelf life. That is why white rice is recommended as opposed to brown rice, which contains more oils and will therefore become rancid more quickly. Unaided, white rice will store for a few years, but placed into a mylar bag and heat-sealed with an oxygen absorber, it can last 30 years, some say indefinitely. And remember, beggars can't be choosers. Not everything is inedible just because it has begun to spoil. If bugs have hatched in your rice (which shouldn't be possible in an oxygen-free mylar bag), remember that bugs are edible. Ask Klaus Schwab.

Rice can still be affordably purchased in bulk at this time; 25 lbs for about $10 where I'm from. For relatively little money, one can acquire hundreds of pounds (thousands is better) of rice, which would serve as an excellent base of carbohydrates for meat and garden vegetables to be incorporated into. I'd stock up on salt and bullion as well for flavor. Salt can be purchased in bulk, and being a preservative it will never expire.

Rice and lentils are dry, thus easy to store long term. Not so with meat or vegetables. There are ways wet foods can be preserved using salt and dehydration, but canning seems to be the most effective, many experienced canners even claiming that canned items remain edible almost indefinitely, though they may slowly become mushier and less nutritional over time. Ergo, a canning book and some mason jars may be a good investment.

Water is easier in areas that are not arid because it falls from the sky. According to tests, rainwater is generally purer than ground water, well water, or municipal water. It can be easily harvested from a roof, diverted from gutters into collection containers. It will naturally carry some dirt and debris with it, however, this will be cleared by the filtering process prior to drinking. A gravity filter from companies like Big Berkey or Alexapure can be purchased, or one can be made by drilling some holes in the bottom of a bucket, filling it with 4 inches of gravel, 4 inches of sand, 4 inches of crushed charcoal (which removes toxins), and another 4 inches of sand topped with a little gravel for good measure. By the time the water filters through all of this and drains into a separate collection bucket below, it should be potable. If filtering extremely dirty water, pool shock without algaecide is shelf-stable (but be careful with this) and effectively kills undesirables. It is said that the chlorine can be aerated by pouring the water back and forth between glasses, though I have not tried this.

How tragic it would be for such preparations to be made only to be confiscated by local authorities under the auspices of a national emergency, which will have almost certainly been declared in the event you are resorting to consuming your food stores. Those who have diligently prepared will be denounced as greedy hoarders and blamed for the starvation of those who chose to remain in denial and do nothing. Have no doubt that in such a situation the authorities would be entering homes to confiscate any "excess" as has been done historically. For the greater good, of course. If I am not mistaken, provisions for this very thing have already been made in United States legislation and likely in most other nations.

It is very risky then to prepare without a good hiding spot. Dig holes. Build false walls. Fill floorboards. If gardening, stage your plots in irregular shapes and scatter them to appear as natural foliage and don't mow your lawn. Bury a cistern for drinking water. Bury an airtight container to conceal firearms. Develop an ambiguous living space in an attic or basement. Make your home appear unappealing. Stage it to lend the appearance of it having already been ransacked and seal off a room with an obscured entrance to serve as your primary living quarters. If you have well-treed acreage, drag a camper off the beaten path and further obscure it with camo netting and/or fake Christmas trees if necessary. Humans are naturally lazy, and even trained henchmen will not likely exert themselves more than needed, so they're more likely to search your home than your woods.

Don't listen to the know-it-alls who claim you need to have the skills of a Navy Seal to survive. Skills make it easier, but they aren't often necessary. Homeless people survive with nearly nothing all the time. Still, knowledge is power, and it could be lifesaving to procure some how-to information pertaining to foraging in your specific geographic location, practicing medicine off-grid, fishing, hunting, skinning, butchering, building, gardening, canning, and any number of things. The bounty of knowledge that can be printed from the internet is nearly endless. Best to acquire it while we still have a functional internet.

Different locations require different prepping. If you live in a desert, you would likely want a heavy focus on water procurement, whereas if you live in the north, faring subzero temperatures will need to be a consideration. Many Army surplus retailers sell used gear rated for such temperatures. Stay dry while staying warm by ensuring that your base layer is a moisture-wicking material such as wool rather than cotton. Buy a propane heater and stove and/or have a wood-burning stove. Propane will not expire, whereas gasoline will, if there is even any gas to be had in the future. If there isn't, then a gas generator won't do any good, in which case having a solar powered battery (such as a Jackery or your own setup) is a good option. No, it probably won't power your entire house, but it could power an electric griddle, heater, or lights. Depending on the battery, one could power an ice chest long enough to freeze solid blocks of ice which could then be kept in an insulated container and perhaps partially buried to aid in food preservation.

It may be wise to look into seed harvesting/preservation considering our overlords are investing in developing plants that are not seed-bearing, meaning that the only seeds we'll have access to are the GMO seeds bought directly from the very people who have stated their intention to infuse all plants/foods with their nanotechnology. I like potatoes because they're easy, relatively caloric, and you can just set some aside to keep in a dark, cool place until you plant them again next season. I like the Kratky method of non-circulating hydroponic gardening because you can grow food all year with no soil or pests, and no electricity provided you can set the bins in a sunlit area – it's so easy you can watch one Youtube video and have it figured out. And finally, I like pellet guns for quietly plinking birds out of trees, and you can acquire them sans gun registry. Just a few bites of meat provide more calories than entire bowls of greens.

I can't imagine any scenario in which gold and silver lose all value. It is all but certain that it's safer to have precious metals than dollars at this point in time. The digital dollars in my bank account can read all zeros overnight, but silver in my hand will remain in my hand whether there's a "cyber attack" (false flag) or not. If a dollar goes to zero, it becomes mere paper. If gold artificially drops in value, it's still an element on the periodic table and has intrinsic worth as it always has throughout all human history. That said, in certain scenarios, basic bartering items like ammo may be worth their weight in gold. There may come a time when a shotgun is worth more than a Ferrari, which can be rendered useless by an EMP or gasoline shortage unlike a firearm.

Things like silver, gold, diamonds, and dollars are only as valuable as the goods they potentially represent. It wouldn't make much sense to amass silver and gold to barter it for water filters, food, and tools during a collapse when you could just amass water filters, food, and tools now without the additional unnecessary step of procuring the precious metals. Though I can't recommend holding onto dollars when for most people those dollars are digital and therefore insecure, one could get their dollars out of the bank by purchasing preps first, and then after all preparations are made, putting any excess dollars into precious metals could be considered.

Prepping requires foresight. By the time calamity strikes, it's too late. It requires a bit of prescience to stock up on necessities even while everything is relatively rosy and peaceful. But it doesn't necessarily need to be financially risky. All the following are shelf-stable, will generally retain or gain value, and can be used 20 years from now if nothing ever happens: firearms, ammunition, propane (+stove/heater/etc.), cold-rated clothing, knives, tools, water filters, and the list goes on. These are good to have regardless of there being a global takeover by the New World Order elites. Spending hundreds or thousands on preps might sound overwhelming, but over the course of decades it isn't as much as it seems, and as the price of goods is likely to continue climbing into the stratosphere, it may be more frugal to purchase as much as possible right now rather than paying double for the same thing next year, however, only you can make that call as you are more familiar with your current situation than anyone else.

There are many more things to consider, like the importance of building community or staying at least a few miles away from any major highways, but there are much better resources than myself for further considerations. I tend to often recommend Mike Adams as he is a long-time prepper and offers his knowledge for free:

https://www.resilientprepping.com/ReaderRegistration-Downloads.asp?Subscriber=True

And here's a resource for spiritual preparation as you'll eventually die no matter what happens:

Bible

It will forever be a mystery to me how much focus we dedicate to this ephemeral life that is so brief in comparison with the infinitely longer afterlife that goes largely ignored despite the potential for unimaginable consequences for doing so. If you don't believe there's an afterlife, you better be pretty damn certain of it, but you aren't because it isn't possible to be. The common retort to this is, "Well, you can't be certain of an afterlife either" which is incorrect. One can experience a thing that exists (and very many people have experienced God undeniably) but one cannot experience the nonexistence of a thing. So rationality lies on the side of the Theist. It's not my intent to alienate Atheists, but spiritual preparation is far more important than mortal physical preparation, and to omit it from any discussion of prep work would be a disservice.

Stopping the onslaught of globalism and its green antihuman antimoral religion would require a complete uprooting of the mind control operation known as the education system, a total cleansing of corrupt governments across the globe, the annihilation of the entertainment (programming) industry, and the obliteration of the news media along with Big Tech social media. In essence, all the people and institutions that hold all the money and power would need to be overtaken, and although we, the people of the world, have the numbers, we don't have the willingness to reject the decadence pressed upon us that is necessary to make it happen. Too many have fallen in love with their servitude. Gee, I'd love to ditch Propagandaflix, but it has such good shows! I know the NFL supports far Left globalist agendas, but I can't miss a football game!

No, I believe our only recourse at this point is to prepare for the fallout of humanity's collective apathy to evil. The tsunami is coming, and it will eventually crash onto our shores, survivable only by having anticipated its arrival and adequately prepared. I hope I'm wrong. If I am, I have lost nothing by preparing as I can use or sell everything I've purchased. I've only gained peace and confidence in my future. Those living under the shadow of the tsunami may not be aware of how bleak their futures are, but those of us with foresight and awareness may remain optimistic about our personal futures regardless of what transpires in the world if only we are successful in separating ourselves from it.

Newsletter 5 – A Hill To Die On

August 17, 2022

As the COVID-19 brainwashing gained traction I had to make a decision as to where I would draw the line. I could be stalwart and declare to my employer that I will not be wearing a mask, but the outcome would have been termination resulting in a significant financial loss inhibiting my ability to invest in necessary future preparations. And for what? It would have effected no change. All my colleagues would still be forced to wear their masks and I would be out of a job. I can deal with an occasional facemask in order to provide for my loved ones. What I cannot do, is allow the globalist government to rape my body with Luciferian technology. For me, forced vaccination is where to draw the line. That is the hill to die on.

At my workplace, the encroaching mandate seemed inevitable. It was happening at many other facilities. The propaganda coming from the state that employs me was incessant and filled with lies and condescending reprimands directed toward those disinclined toward having their bodily autonomy usurped. I could barely stand it. Other similar state agencies were purging their unvaccinated employees and I knew we were next. But by some loophole, they were unable to pull the trigger after all.

Nevertheless, having been so enraged at the injustice of our foolish leadership using threats and coercion to recklessly endorse a potentially deadly science experiment, I felt an obligation to counter their lies with the truth, understanding it would end my career with the state. I began to write an email that I intended to send to as many state employees as possible. Being a combination of naïve and technologically unsavvy, I was unable to achieve this as I learned there are safeguards in place to prevent it. I would only be able to send the finished product to my own work site, and since the vast majority of the employees on site had already taken the shot, it would have fallen on deaf ears. Now I was back to my mask logic: I could stand for my beliefs and send the email to my own people, but it would have accomplished nothing but my termination. Had the state decided to purge the unvaccinated from the service line in which I work, I would have sent it on my way out anyway, but at the penultimate moment we were spared of this pseudoscientific authoritarianism and the email was left unsent.

That said, I hate to be wasteful so I'm sharing it here as the facts remain relevant and can still be referenced today if one were to feel so inclined.

Greetings!

Since our leaders seem to enjoy taking political stances while not-so-discreetly impressing them upon their employees (which is shameful and inappropriate for any employer) and sharing their opinions without providing facts, I thought I would help them out with the fact part.

According to the state's FAQ regarding vaccines, "virtually all hospitalizations and deaths continue to be among the unvaccinated." That's interesting since recently in Vermont, 75% of the people who died of COVID-19 were vaccinated. And that's not an anomaly. Israel, the world's most vaccinated nation, has the highest number of cases per million in the world. According to a study from the Francis Crick Institute in the United Kingdom, that is because Pfizer's COVID-19 vaccine destroys T-cells, weakening the immune system. But you wouldn't need to reference the study to know that because according to Pfizer's own scientists, the vaccines decimate the body's natural immunity. This has already been openly reported.

Waterford has the highest vaccination rate in all of Ireland at 99.7% vaccinated as of September 2021, and it also has the highest rate of COVID infection. You should be starting to see a trend.

A CDC study examining a COVID-19 outbreak that started July 3rd in Provincetown, Mass., involving 469 cases found that three-quarters of cases occurred in fully vaccinated people (the same percentage noted in the Vermont example above). Data from Public Health England demonstrates higher rates of not only infection, but death, among the fully vaccinated (safe and effective). This is further corroborated by data from Israel's Ministry of Health. Still, our leaders tell us to "trust the science" and get vaccinated, while it is the vaccine hesitant that are trusting *actual* science rather than political/scientific TV personalities. On that note, according to researchers at Carnegie Mellon University, PhD's are the most vaccine hesitant demographic. While people with no scientific understanding are screaming at everyone to "trust the science", *actual* scientists who are speaking out against these vaccines are being obfuscated, censored, and deplatformed.

The first cases of the Omicron variant in Africa (and MN) occurred within the vaccinated. In fact, according to the CDC, about 8 in 10 cases of Omicron occur within the vaccinated. Still we are hearing that this is a "pandemic of the unvaccinated", though the data clearly indicates otherwise. Even anecdotally, one can observe that this is nonsense. Look around you. Who is getting sick? Mostly vaccinated people (T-cell reduction, remember). Of my coworkers who have come down with COVID most recently, the vast majority were fully vaccinated – and no, that does not align with the ratio of vaccinated to unvaccinated in our workplace, so the argument, "that's because there are more vaccinated people" is not legitimate (it isn't in any case – just think about it for a minute).

To speak more to that point, data from Taiwan demonstrates that as of October 7th vaccine deaths had exceeded COVID deaths with vaccine deaths totaling 852 (safe and effective) as opposed to COVID deaths totaling 844 – a classic example of "the cure is worse than the disease". Only 20% of the population in Taiwan is vaccinated, therefore, these numbers do not reflect the proportion of vaccinated to unvaccinated, which remember, would be a poor argument anyway. Before the vaccines were introduced to Taiwan in early March, there had only been 12 COVID deaths.

Recently, a news station reached out to social media users to solicit stories about their unvaccinated friends and relatives becoming ill. While they received almost none of the responses they had hoped for, nearly all the responses (thousands upon thousands of them) were from people reporting incidents in which their fully vaccinated peers became remarkably ill, and in many cases, passed away.

Johns Hopkins's Dr. Makary states that the data on natural immunity are overwhelming, that natural immunity is 27 times more effective than vaccinated immunity, which is supported by 16 studies. Maybe that's why 77.7% of COVID deaths in Illinois reported the last week in October were of vaccinated people.

If this is what a successful vaccine looks like, I'd hate to see what an unsuccessful one looks like. Don't let it escape your notice that the CDC has changed the definition of *vaccine* to accommodate the inefficacy of the COVID-19 vaccines. Conveniently, now a vaccine isn't something that prevents one from becoming ill but is instead something that decreases the severity of symptoms (though the COVID-19 vaccines don't even do that – the narrative says they do, the data says they don't).

According to the CDC, deaths from the COVID-19 vaccines have exceeded 16,000 (it's much higher now), however, according to a Harvard study, only about 1% of adverse events are actually reported, so do the math. The CDC also reports a litany of adverse events. Still they parrot "safe and effective" ad nauseum while providing data to contradict their own narrative. Gaslighting at its finest.

Dr. Robert Malone, inventor of the mRNA technology (with patents to show for it) that is being used in Moderna's and Pfizer's COVID-19 vaccines, stated that this technology should never be introduced to the human body and in fact those who are subjected to it are more susceptible to variants and have a higher risk of disease and even death, which is corroborated by the data (again, see Public Health England, CDC, etc).

The state's memo on vaccine side effects that was sent out in August was grossly incomplete. Actual adverse events listed by the FDA Safety Surveillance for COVID-19 Vaccines are as follows: Guillain-Barre Syndrome, Acute disseminated encephalomyelitis, Transverse Myelitis, Encephalitis/meningitis/encephalomyelitis, convulsions/seizures, stroke, narcolepsy and cataplexy, anaphylaxis, acute myocardial infarction, myocarditis/pericarditis, autoimmune disease, deaths, pregnancy and birth outcomes, other acute demyelinating diseases, non-anaphylactic allergic reactions, thrombocytopenia, disseminated intravascular coagulation, venous thromboembolism, arthritis and arthralgia/joint pain, Kawasaki disease, Multisystem Inflammatory Syndrome in children, and vaccine enhanced disease. It then states that the list is subject to change, which can be best interpreted as "more to come", not less.

Cardiac events within vaccinated professional soccer players has increased to 66 times beyond the average. Not 66%, 66 times. That's 6,600%. And the official explanation for this is that it is simply a coincidence or that COVID is to blame, though this increase in mortality was not present until after the vaccines were mandated.

Just prior to the advent of Omicron, NPR offered a detailed report on our nation's emergency rooms being overwhelmed with seriously ill patients, though only a very few with COVID. What a mystery. I'll spell it out: V-A-C-C-I-N-E I-N-J-U-R-I-E-S. Overwhelmed emergency rooms? No problem, we'll just fire all the people that can appropriately manage that. You know, the ones we were calling heroes a few months ago.

When you have one of these many adverse events, remember the state assured you the vaccine was "safe" and actively coerced you into taking it. Then give the Liberty Counsel or Thomas More Law Center a call so they can deal with the state accordingly. Find and save every state email assuring you of vaccine safety.

If our leaders really cared about "doing no harm" as they claim, they would immediately discontinue their reckless promotion of these vaccines in consideration of all the very harmful side effects, including death, that even the manufacturers acknowledge. They would cite facts rather than coercive and errant opinions. But facts are the enemy of their narrative, which is why their communications are devoid of any. That's ok though, I did their job for them and provided some for you, though there are many, many more that I omitted for the sake of brevity.

Trust the science.

Reuters. (December 10, 2021). *Most Reported U.S. Omicron Cases Have Hit the Fully Vaccinated – CDC.* https://www.reuters.com/world/us/most-reported-us-omicron-cases-have-hit-fully-vaccinated-cdc-2021-12-10/

Public Health England. (June 25, 2021). *SARS-CoV-2 Variants of Concern and Variants Under Investigation in England.* https://assets.publishing.service.gov.uk/government/uploads/system/uploads/attachment_data/file/1001354/Variants_of_Concern_VOC_Technical_Briefing_17.pdf

NPR. (October 26, 2021). *ERs are now swamped with seriously ill patients – but many don't even have COVID.* https://www.npr.org/sections/health-shots/2021/10/26/1046432435/ers-are-now-swamped-with-seriously-ill-patients-but-most-dont-even-have-covid

Francis Crick Institute. (June 3, 2021). *Pfizer-BioNTech vaccine recipients have lower antibody levels targeting the Delta variant than other SARS-CoV-2 variants.* https://www.crick.ac.uk/news/2021-06-03_pfizer-biontech-vaccine-recipients-have-lower-antibody-levels-targeting-the-delta-variant-than-other-sars-cov-2-variants

The Irish Post. (October 18, 2021). *Waterford has Ireland's second highest incidence rate despite the fact that 99.7% are fully vaccinated.* https://www.irishpost.com/news/waterford-has-irelands-second-highest-covid-19-incidence-rate-despite-fact-99-7-of-residents-are-fully-vaccinated-222363

WCVB5. (July 30,2021). *CDC Analysis shows 75% of Provincetown cases occurred in vaccinated individuals.* https://www.wcvb.com/article/cdc-analysis-shows-74-of-provincetown-cases-occurred-in-vaccinated-individuals/37182364

Medical Trend. (November 4, 2021). *Taiwan deaths from COVID-19 vaccination exceeds death from COVID-19.* https://medicaltrend.org/2021/10/10/taiwan-death-from-covid-19-vaccination-exceeds-death-from-covid-19/

Newsletter 6 – A Tempest

August 31, 2022

I was recently featured on a podcast (CramerSez) during which the question of what I thought might occur pre- or post-election was asked of me, at which I can only speculate. A major red wave is anticipated this November, precipitated by the disgust that the American people have for the destruction that blue policies have wrought. The Democrat party is well aware of this and are desperate to ensure that it does not occur as it would interrupt the onslaught of Globalism that has been creating such havoc for the past two years. It is a popular thing to say that there is no difference between the Left and the Right, however, it is the Leftist platform that is spearheading the tenets of the New Religion of the NWO: child grooming is a virtue, abortion is freedom, gender is only a construct, it's loving to leave borders wide open, forced vaccination is good, lockdowns are good, America has an obligation to give all of its money to Ukraine while veterans and people in need remain neglected, homosexuality is virtuous but cisgender males are inherently evil, it's enlightened to teach children that their white skin makes them evil and to teach black children that they are universally hated, efficient energy should be eradicated, the polar ice caps are melting despite all evidence that they are not, free speech should be silenced, the 2nd amendment should be abolished. This is the doctrine of the Left. No, the Left and the Right are not the same. The Left is a representation of Globalism while the right is a representation of Nationalism. The Left are progressive. That is, they seek to progress away from traditional values. What are traditional values? Whether you like it or not, traditional values are Christian values. The Right are conservative. That is, they seek to *conserve* traditional values. In this manner, it becomes apparent that what we are looking at is a battle between the pro-Christian Right and the anti-Christian Left, whose every value is a separation from

Biblical tenets – those tenets that are necessary for the healthy functioning of any free nation.

The Democrats cannot allow a red wave to sweep the nation and interfere with all the authoritarian groundwork they've laid, just as they could not allow the 2020 election to result in anything other than a puppet president that would unquestioningly fulfill their every order. This is not a plug for Trump. I have no allegiance to a man who still promotes a deadly "vaccine" despite the overwhelming damage it has caused. My opinion is that the Globalists cannot abide a Republican majority House and Senate just as they could not abide a President they couldn't control for another 4 years which resulted in a very blatantly fraudulent 2020 election. For them to achieve their Sustainable Development Goals (Agenda 2030), an American President that actively endorses their aims and performs as directed is necessary. Considering the lengths they went to usurp the current Presidency, it seems likely they may interfere with the midterm elections as well. The question is, in what manner?

Some believe that lockdowns will again be imposed in order to justify the use of mail-in ballots, which are very insecure and easy to manipulate as we have seen. This could be a pandemic lockdown or a climate lockdown. Both are scenarios discussed by our leadership. Though people seem to be over the lockdowns and may not comply, the mail-in ballots would likely be instituted with or without public consent.

Another scenario spoken of by Globalist overlords is that of a widespread cyber crash. This, Klaus Schwab assures us, would be among the most devastating things that could occur. No internet means no business means no fuel means no food means pandemonium. This would of course result in a national emergency. I still find it strange that the Cyber Polygon group had planned, then cancelled, their meeting for

July 8th, the same date that Canada experienced a widespread shutdown of ATM's and internet banking services. I maintain that Cyber Polygon cancelled their public-facing meeting in favor of a cyber attack dry run (though the Rogers incident in WEF-controlled Canada was not attributed to a cyber-attack, the impact was consistent with one), which leads me to speculate that perhaps they're in a hurry and their schedule did not allow for yet another meeting with no action. Perhaps the eagerly awaited great cyber crash is closer than we care to think.

One scenario that many dismiss is the possibility of a world war, perhaps reaching nuclear levels. The skeptics say this is not possible because of the principle of M.A.D, or Mutually Assured Destruction, that is, if one nation launches a nuclear weapon, then nuclear detonation will be visited upon them in return. Perhaps this was true when nations tended toward sovereignty, but when there are inside players that have no allegiance to the nations they govern, and in fact they actively seek to destroy their own nations because their allegiance (and income/power) comes from Globalists, M.A.D is negated. In this case, launching a nuclear weapon does not necessarily guarantee the same fate being returned because it could be the result of a mutual agreement between an external threat and a traitorous government, such as a president having highly lucrative dealings with the leader of another rival country.

The United States' National Strategy for Countering Domestic Terrorism released in June of 2021 discreetly identifies whites, Christians, and Conservatives as domestic extremists and anticipates terror attacks from these groups. This lays the groundwork for provocateured events or false flag operations that they can use as a precedent for shutting down free elections and/or carrying forward their attack on patriotic Americans with traditional values as the IRS has historically done (and are now recruiting 87,000 agents trained to kill Americans). I would not be surprised to see a staged terror attack precede the election that the Democrats would then exploit for Globalist gain.

Perhaps nothing will happen at all. Maybe the election will take place as expected and the world will continue its slow boil to destruction at a steady pace. Or perhaps there really is a silent movement of White Hats that are on the verge of destroying the Globalists. Though I find that unlikely, nothing is impossible in these unprecedented times so a preparatory approach remains wise. Expect the worst, hope for the best.

Despite the state of things, there is no need to fear for those of us who choose to separate ourselves from the system that is emerging, however, for those that willingly align themselves with it, there is just cause for fear because they choose to do so potentially at the expense of their souls.

A woman I know told me a dream she had. She was in something like a large gymnasium with many people who were being helped by men in uniform. Contingents of people would be led out of the main area by these uniformed men and would not be seen again. Though the men were there to help, this woman began to feel fearful of the situation that she was in and she went to the door to exit the building. When she opened it, there was a raging storm outside but there was a strange relief in it. Though the storm was violent, she felt safer on her own with the rain and lightning than in the building where everyone's needs were apparently being provided for by what appeared to be military or government officials.

The moral of course is not to fear the storm. Rather be skeptical when our rulership offers a helping hand to save us from it.

Newsletter 7 – To Thin The Veil

September 9, 2022

If you're receiving this message, you likely believe that Big Pharma is a testament to the greedy corruption of mankind. The COVID-19 sham vaccines have demonstrated not only this corruption, but also a deep evil that is threaded throughout our corporate government. Does this evil stop at the J&J, Moderna, and Pfizer eugenics injections, or does it go deeper? Perhaps we should never have trusted the flu vaccines either. Perhaps antidepressants, anxiolytics, and various other drugs should always have been regarded with much greater scrutiny than they have been. In this world where others are taken advantage of for personal gain is it far-fetched to believe that an industry that profits from illness may be something less than benevolent, or is it illogical not to?

Now that it is becoming increasingly more evident that we are being lied to on a regular basis, we should consider what else we have been lied to about. Are the speculative timelines that our scientific community has surmised for the origin and development of this planet accurate? Is it true that a rogue gunman assassinated JFK? Are eggs really bad for your health and low-fat foods good? These are fair questions in a world in which we are reared into a particular narrative that our society fails to adequately scrutinize. It's almost as if a spell has been cast over the entire world and we walk about in a daze believing whatever we're told.

It was once less commonly known that *pharmacy* is a word derived from the ancient Greek *pharmakeia*, which is synonymous with sorcery, though current events have popularized this knowledge to some extent. The connection between drugs and witchcraft is evident from shamanic spirit quests of old to current channeling practices in this modern age. Many people around the world describe seeing aliens, serpents, or elves (at times referred to as *machine elves*) while under the influence. In their suggestible drug-addled state, these experiencers tend to be told similar things by these beings, such as that there are too many people on the planet, that humans need to merge with machines, or that Jesus is not the Messiah. One experiencer described a time that he mentioned Jesus to the elves, who responded very angrily. Others have reported taking the powerful hallucinogen ayahuasca/DMT as a group who subsequently all described having seen the same entity (hint: if multiple people see the same thing, it's not a hallucination).

It is suspected that perhaps the veil of perception between this world and the next is somehow upheld by our consciousness, many speculating that the pineal gland in the brain is responsible for this phenomenon. Philosopher Rene Des Cartes, known for his existential conclusion, *I think therefore I am*, was a proponent of substance dualism, that is, the belief that the brain does not produce consciousness, but rather consciousness and the brain/body are separate, i.e., humans have souls. He referred to the pineal gland as "the seat of the soul", that singular point at which soul joins body.

Not all drugs influence the mind and body the same way. As a clinical supervisor in a treatment facility for the chemically dependent and mentally ill, I can assure you the number of clients we see for drugs like marijuana, MDMA, or hallucinogens is very low. The bulk of our clientele arrive due mostly to addiction to methamphetamine, heroin/opiates, or alcohol. Opiates appear to result in the most overdoses but are generally less damaging to the body than the other two. Withdrawal from heroin is not fatal without preexisting conditions, whereas withdrawal from alcohol is. Alcohol is by far the deadliest drug and wreaks havoc on the body even more so than meth. Of meth I have most often heard statements like, "It turned me into a monster" or "It's the devil's drug" and is more likely to result in psychosis.

Suffice it to say that there is a vast array of mind-altering substances in the world that impact the human being in various ways – mind, body, and soul – and they could all be described as sorcerous in one way or another. Many would not dispute this as it pertains to illicit substances, but what of the medicinal drugs offered by the pharmaceutical industry? Is there any difference? Consider that heroin is an opiate and meth is an amphetamine, both of which are used medicinally in prescription drugs such as Adderall and Vicodin. But these are known drugs of abuse. What about medicines for anxiety, depression, blood pressure, indigestion, cough/cold, or cancer?

Assuredly there are beneficial medications. Medicines are merely derivatives of the earth. Most are developed from the properties of certain plants. Gout can be treated just with cherry juice. Surely we're not going to relegate cherries to sorcery. The human body is of the earth and it is intended to be interactive with the earth and what the earth produces. We of course will perish without consuming things of the earth which our bodies then integrate. Animal and plant life becomes our life as they sustain us. Plants are medicine.

It seems what distinguishes a substance as pharmakeia may be a combination of psychoactive properties and the intent behind its use. For instance, if one wishes not to open a doorway to spiritual entities, steering clear of dimethyltryptamine (ayahuasca) would be wise. But there are other less extreme substances, such as antidepressants, that may warrant some skepticism as well even if they don't yield such dramatic hallucinogenic results.

The most common antidepressants are SSRI's or selective serotonin reuptake inhibitors. These were developed on the premise that depression is an organic brain disorder caused by insufficient serotonin, the neurotransmitter responsible for mood stabilization among other things. This premise has its own premise, that of epiphenomenalism which is the antithesis to the substance dualism espoused by Des Cartes. Epiphenomenalism postulates that consciousness derives from the brain. There is no soul. That is what medicine is predicated on. But if that premise is incorrect and mental/emotional maladies do in fact result from the nonphysical, then should we have such implicit trust in pharmaceutical remedies that are manufactured on a faulty premise?

Most of the time when I ask a client how their antidepressant is working, they respond with something like, *not at all* or *I think it kind of helps,* which is a placebo response if I ever heard one. Seldom, if ever, do I hear that it's a total game changer and they are in such a better place since taking them. I had long suspected that antidepressants are ineffective since I reject the idea that the brain produces consciousness and emotions. I wondered why depression diagnoses are at an all time high when antidepressant prescriptions are also at an all time high. If antidepressants were effective, shouldn't we see a negative correlation? Shouldn't the rate of depression decrease with the increase of prescribed antidepressants? And why is nobody asking this question?

But somebody finally did. This year, 2022, a published study by Joanna Moncrieff, et al, concluded that there is "no consistent evidence of there being an association between serotonin and depression". Why did it take the scientific community so long to conclude what has always been obvious? Because science is a religion. Because John Rockefeller created the modern medical community to be lucrative via pharmaceuticals and forced pharmaceutical propaganda into medical education where it remains today.

Because Big Pharma has been making billions from SSRI prescriptions for decades.

Moncrieff's study will likely result in no change. The pharmaceutical dogma is too ingrained. Indoctrinated prescribers and adherents of epiphenomenalist scientism will come barking in defense of these often useless, and even damaging, "medicines".

There is vast diversity among human physiology and far be it from me to declare that antidepressants have never been of benefit to any single human being. It's possible that they do have a discernible positive impact on some. It's also possible that the placebo effect may influence an individual to feel better just knowing they're receiving a treatment of some kind. If it's working for you, keep doing what you're doing. This isn't medical advice.

Though today people seem to regard drug use as largely a modern phenomenon, it has been ubiquitous throughout history and just like ancient nature worship and today's green movement, it is closely associated with human destruction. Historically, hallucinogenic drug use can be correlated to widespread human sacrifice. Upon taking hallucinogens, the priest classes of many cultures began to believe that the gods were telling them to sacrifice their children, almost as if these drugs opened a doorway to demonic genocidal influence (see J.R. Irvin's work for more information). Toxicology results show that ritual drug use was involved with Incan human sacrifices that took place atop Ampato Mountain in Peru. Aztecs would sacrifice their children to their gods, roll their bodies down the temple steps, and cannibalize the corpses. When Cortez arrived, many surrounding tribes were fed up with the constant death, and gladly accepted Christianity over the human slaughter offered by the pagan system which is the default religion of Godless people. When The Creator instructed Abraham to sacrifice his son Isaac, Abraham didn't appear to blink an eye because that was the standard practice when dealing with "gods". But the message that *THE* God was sending to Abraham is that He is not a murderous false god, that the true God is the pro-human force in the world, and that human sacrifice is not something His people are ever to practice, and He then provided a ram to be sacrificed in Isaac's stead.

As a part of the CIA's MKUltra program, psychedelic drugs were promoted to the American people. Naturally, a government would desire its people to be suggestible for greater ease of subservience. Perhaps they've learned that powerful hallucinogens are a bit too over-the-top and they've now opted for a more subtle control mechanism. As we have seen the relationship between government and the pharmaceutical industry, and we have an awareness that human beings can be better controlled via chemical influence, and we understand that governments seek power and control of the people above all else, perhaps some skepticism even of "legitimate" drugs is warranted. Perhaps we are dealing with the soma of Huxley's Brave New World. Most mass shooters in recent history appear to have been taking antidepressants, and more than a few have had ties to the FBI prior to their shooting. It's almost as if the chemical softening of their brains enabled deep state groomers to influence them to commit acts of violence.

I take medication every day for heartburn. I've tried weaning it down. I've tried natural remedies like apple cider vinegar. I've tried changing my diet. There seems to be no alternative: either I take omeprazole every day or I live with constant heartburn for my entire life, ultimately eroding my esophagus. It's interesting how few medications actually resolve a malady rather than just treating the symptoms thereby engendering dependence which of course is lucrative. In my opinion, medications do have their place, I just think it's wise to consider their source particularly when they are formulated to influence the mind or emotions. As for me, I will never allow myself to be injected with anything the Luciferian corporate elite want in my body.

Oh, on that note, I often hear people with vaccine regret wondering if they'll be okay as long as they don't get boosted. I have a good deal of empathy for these people and want to reassure them, but I don't know if I can as all I have are opinions and there's much we just don't know yet. But I can offer this – the tenacity with which our death cult leaders promote boosters tells me they want as much of the mystery mRNA substance inside as many people as possible. After all, they're still working intently on infusing GMO foods with mRNA so we can be "vaccinated" even when we eat. To me, that makes little sense unless the overall effect is cumulative. By that logic it seems as though someone who only took one or two jabs would be better off than someone who took five, but of course there are no guarantees in life. We could die in a freak accident at any moment. Actually, I take it back – there is one guarantee in life: death is guaranteed (excepting rapture). Therefore, the most important thing in anyone's life is to work out their salvation with fear and trembling. The epiphenomenalists are incorrect. We will experience an afterlife. It's up to us to determine which one to aspire toward.

Choose wisely!

Newsletter 8 – The Battles Rage On

October 10, 2022

It's been a while since my last newsletter. The war continues to escalate as pipelines are sabotaged, Russian submarines armed with nuclear missiles are on the move, technology continues to be weaponized by globalists (such as vaccine-delivering mosquitos and mRNA-infused food products), the war against free speech rages on, and the media continues to lie about it all.

The globalist elite already have control over all the primary information outlets: education, mainstream media, social media, Hollywood, and major corporations. However, although they have made every effort to control the internet, it is a more difficult beast to tame and they remain threatened by it, therefore, they are doubling down on their desperate attempts to monopolize the narrative. In case you haven't noticed, search engine optimization has been turned against the people, yielding primarily state-sanctioned narratives in the results of online searches. Page after page, the same few sources are endlessly repeated. Perhaps the following remark from Melissa Fleming, the United Nations Under-Secretary General for Global Communications can provide some clarity:

"If you Google climate change, at the top of your search you will get all kinds of UN resources. We started this partnership when we were shocked to see that when we Googled 'climate change' we were getting all kinds of distorted information right at the top... We own the science and we think the world should know it."

In other words, they discovered that their narrative was falling apart as people with common sense were questioning their lies and even daring to go so far as to publish evidence that contradicted their edicts, and so their tongues had to be torn out. Of course, we knew this war on internet free speech would result in such things because they've published multiple white papers that stated that is precisely what they intended to do. Perhaps then their other stated intentions – such as mobilizing local law enforcement to detain free-speaking people – should be taken seriously as well.

The war on biology also rages on. Newsbreak recently published an article claiming there is a "mysterious village" in the Dominican Republic in which all babies are born female but later in puberty develop male genitalia. But maybe it's not so mysterious. How could such a phenomenon be confined to a single village? One explanation is that their water supply is contaminated just as Atrazine (a hormone disruptor used to inhibit reproduction in fish hatcheries) has been found in the water supply in the United States. We can know for certain that the US government has been heavily invested in conducting experimentation of this nature since at least 1974 because that is what is clearly stated in the NSSM-200.

At least they've finally let up on trying to inject mRNA into everyone, right? Or have they just graduated to more surreptitious means as trust in Western medicine continues to wane? That's what I would put my money on as mosquitos are being genetically modified into flying syringes and infusing spinach, lettuce, and other foods with mRNA is being openly praised. Not only that, but flu shots will now contain mRNA. Flu shots without mRNA were bad enough. Though at my former workplace I was bombarded with "science" that assured me that the flu shot does not make people sick, my observations said otherwise as so many people around me fell ill immediately following vaccination. Now at my current workplace the infection prevention czar is baffled that vaccination rates for the flu last year were lower than ever! Hard to imagine being that clueless.

Thanks to Project Veritas, CNN Technical Director, Charlie Chester was caught on camera acknowledging that the new narrative focus in the media would not be Trump or COVID, but climate change. This is apparent enough as the COVID narrative has always been tied to climate change. In fact, Schwab's Great Reset book is almost as much about climate change as it is about COVID, praising lockdowns as being good for the planet as they resulted in decreased carbon emissions. Furthermore, Schwab stated that COVID-19 was the test of global compliance as billions of people adhered to authoritarian mandates which demonstrated to him that lockdowns for climate change can now be implemented.

As the war on energy pushes forward, rolling blackouts are anticipated for much of Europe this winter, but may also impact parts of North America as well. It seems likely that rolling blackouts and climate lockdowns would initially be minimized in the fashion of "two weeks to flatten the curve" to mitigate retaliation but then be expanded moving forward.

As economies collapse, talk of central bank digital currencies increases. As practiced in some parts of the world, digital currencies would be linked to a social credit score which would be calculated based not only on carbon allowances but on solidarity with the latest thing, be it BLM, LGBT, trusting "science" or whatever they demand. It would likely not be only punitive, but also coercive: *New exclusive offer this month only! Change your profile pic to this rainbow image to celebrate LGBTQIA+ child gender reassignment and get 25 credits FREE!*

Just a hunch.

Gender disruption and identity confusion is merely an antecedent for the fully realized transhumanist agenda, but folks like you are probably already aware of that.

Compliance with the antichrist agenda will be rewarded just as it currently is amongst major corporations. Why would corporations like Netflix and the NFL push woke trash when nobody likes it and they lose customers as a result? Aren't capitalists supposed to cater to their consumer base? They do it because Satanic organizations like Black Rock and Vanguard subsidize them for their compliance. Though their public-facing numbers indicate a loss in revenue, they are actually making more money for promoting the anti-family, anti-human, anti-God agenda. I can think of no other reason any company would continue to willfully sustain such considerable losses by producing products that they know their customers hate.

Though the mainstream narrative persists that Russia sabotaged its own Nord Stream pipeline, this makes little sense and no evidence for this accusation has been presented. Meanwhile, it is claimed that there is no evidence that the United States had anything to do with the destruction of the Nord Stream pipelines. But there is. State department official Victoria Nuland stated, "If Russia invades Ukraine, one way or another Nord Stream 2 will not move forward" and GOP Senator Ron Johnson has also called for the destruction of the Nord Stream pipelines. President Biden is also on record stating, "...there will be no longer a Nord Stream 2, we will bring an end to it."

Russian intelligence is almost certainly aware that the pipeline attack was carried out by NATO. This is an egregious act of war that further validates that we are in the early stages of World War 3.

Meanwhile, Natural News reports that hundreds of thousands of fully vaccinated people are dying every week according to official government reports. It appears that the damage caused by vaccines is becoming increasingly difficult for the information controllers to suppress as even the CDC has been forced to acknowledge that vaccinated people are more likely to fall ill. In fact, as indicated by insurance companies there has been a 163% increase in death year over year. A recent study out of Taiwan indicates that 29% of vaccinated children have some form of heart condition. Ambulance calls continue to increase month after month with no end in sight. The government and medical community play damage control by issuing public messages that encourage young people – even children – to get their hearts checked and attempt to reassure the public that children suffering heart attacks is perfectly normal and has always been a regular occurrence. It is reported that the Israeli government has been exposed covering up vaccine deaths in children so that they can continue promoting it. The "died suddenly" headlines show no sign of slowing and are no respecter of persons as even prominent figures continue to perish as Coolio recently did.

It can be difficult to ascertain what the biggest threat is in this chaotic world. Is it the potential for the immediate devastation of a nuclear attack? Is it the relatively slower but steadily increasing death by vaccine? Is it a future famine that lies dormant as current food reserves are depleted and food production continues to wane? Is it the water shortages predicted by the UN for 2025? Those who maintain that all the above are tactics used by the government to keep the people in a state of fear could have some credibility concerning the latter threats as they are future projections, however, the realities of an intentionally provoked war and increasing vaccine deaths seem to negate the idea that all the projections of chaos are mere scare tactics with no teeth.

I do not believe we have arrived at the end of all things yet. I do not believe the vaccines are the mark of the beast (though I think they're a precursor). I do not believe that Jesus will arrive within the decade. I do believe that the world has entered a new season, the beginning of the end. But just the beginning. Admittedly, I'm no scholar of end times prophecy, but I believe the Antichrist has yet to rise to power. The war against the saints is not in full swing. Men are not yet dying from fear of what is coming upon the earth. There is more to transpire before the very end is upon us.

Still, most of the world (including Christians) denies the Biblical prophecy that has come to pass and is coming to pass before our very eyes. The drying of the Euphrates must be a coincidence. The building of the 3rd temple is just a metaphor. The Bible doesn't really say there will be a one-world government. Even if one was justified in writing off one of these prophecies, it takes quite an act of faith to dismiss them all even while they can be observed actively occurring. But people allow their desires to drive their beliefs.

No man knows the day or the hour of Christ's return, or the rapture for that matter. No projected specific dates for occasions such as these should be taken seriously, though signs of the times have been given to us so that we may at least discern the season and prepare our hearts accordingly.

There are many who seek to conjure esoteric messages where none exist via gematria, i.e., ascribing a numerical value to a letter and then calculating the letters of a word to equal a number with some cryptic meaning, sometimes interpreted as a meaningful date. If adding the letters doesn't give them an evocative result, they multiply; if multiplication doesn't do the trick, they divide, and so forth until the desired result is achieved. There appears to be no logical basis for calculations such as these, and even if there was, again there is no one who knows the day or the hour of the Lord's return according to Bible prophecy.

Still, we are given signs of the season to guide us which is sufficient for both spiritual and physical preparatory purposes. *Something strange is going on in the world* is an understatement. Those who claim to believe otherwise must be in an extraordinary state of denial similar to the people who are permanently maimed by the vaccine yet still go on to praise the dangerous new technology. Let's not allow ourselves to fall into the same state of denial. Let's not begin to feel comfortable with tyranny. Let's fully reject the evils of this world by embracing Christ, the antithesis of tyranny and the true path to the eternal life that the transhumanist elite so desperately pursue, albeit in the most deluded and futile way possible. Or join the globalist elite in their rejection of Christ and their embrace of the tantalizing empty promises of the world and meet the same end. The choice is ours.

Newsletter 9 – Global Censorship and The End

October 23, 2022

The war on truth rages on as evidenced by the recent purge of content creators on Tik Tok, including myself (new account is @nwo.documents). Just prior to the ban, I had been pondering the state of things as I often do, and I began to consider the implications of censorship. What does it say about where we are at? What does it say about where we're headed?

Freedom of speech demands that all speech be allowed, even if it is untrue. It identifies censorship as inherently dangerous to freedom, even when what is being censored is hateful and evil. But that is not the case today. If hate was being censored it would be dangerous enough, but the situation is more dire than that. It is truth and the promotion of freedom itself that is being censored. My first encounter with this was when I read a Pfizer study verbatim on Youtube and quickly learned that that was strictly forbidden. Reading aloud a document that is readily available on the internet is "misinformation".

What are the implications of dictators not allowing the truth to be spoken? What does it mean when facts are called lies, lies are called truth, and those who dare speak out are shut up, demonetized, legally attacked, and even dragged from their homes and arrested?

If this kind of evil was isolated to a single country it would be dangerous enough, but this is occurring globally. Big tech is the mouthpiece of the globalist agenda, it is more powerful than the leaders of nations, it exerts global control, and it decides what is true. What are the implications of the truth being globally censored? Damnation. No nation can retain its freedoms in such a condition as this. Any nation that does not crush the lies and censorship of social media, mainstream media, education, and government, is absolutely destined for failure.

The situation is far more serious than most care to admit. Some remain blissfully optimistic and maintain that the globalists are in retreat and we are winning! I am currently looking at a headline that reads, "The Globalists are Weaker than They've Ever Been!"

They are? The Dutch government is still pushing toward eradicating farming (as are many other countries), NATO continues to provoke WW3, the CDC continues to promote child murder via mandatory vaccination, economic disaster is inevitable, and I could go on and on and on and on and on. We've gone beyond the tipping point.

Some would rebut, "But people are waking up!"

So what? Have you tried posting about the fact that there is now irrefutable evidence that the vaccines are deadly? Or that migrant children are disappearing by the thousands? Or that climate change alarmism is a lie that will result in millions of deaths? It's not allowed. It's misinformation. It's hate speech. Does it matter whether the entire world is awake or asleep when those in control decide what you can and cannot say? The fact that people are waking up is not indicative that we are winning. If we were winning, we could freely express ourselves online. If we were winning, there would be nobody still in prison simply for being present at the capitol on January 6th. If we were winning, Joe and Hunter Biden would both be on trial due to the irrefutable proof of treason that we had even prior to Joe's usurpation of the presidency. We would not be giving billions to Ukraine against the wishes of the people. The CDC wouldn't dare recommend the death shots for children. Trans child-groomers wouldn't dare show their faces, much less perform drag shows for children. Yet they still do. Because we are not winning. Not at all.

No, we continue to lose. Badly. As the "died suddenly" articles and obituaries accelerate, those sharing them continue to be silenced. Despite the massive amount of evidence that has now accumulated to demonstrate what is true – about the vaccines, about government corruption, about any of it – the globalist narrative remains the strongest. What is the state of our world when evidence no longer matters?

Is it all hopeless then? The Western world praises evil and hates what is good. No, there is no hope for the survival of any Western nation. The West has made its choice. Yet, there is hope for individuals. You can be a survivor in a fallen nation in two easy steps: 1) Do not be a brainwashed idiot that believes the news and implicitly trusts government, and 2) make the necessary preparations that are appropriate for you and your loved ones.

I can't tell you what those preparations should be as I am not familiar with your unique individual situations. As for myself, I have concerns about the future of medical freedom as much of the still-employed medical community remains biased and weaponized against the free-thinking intellectually superior unvaccinated population (further evidence that we are not winning). I find a great deal of utility in medical preparations since removing medical care from dissenters is part of the globalist agenda, therefore, I was elated to learn of a wonderful legal loophole.

I learned that certain manufacturers have formulated fish antibiotics for humans, even forming them into capsules for human ingestion. They knew there was a market for the prepper demographic and they rose to the occasion. This is especially relieving to me as following an extremely painful infection in November of 2020, I became concerned about the possibility of having been rejected by the hospital for being unvaccinated. Untreated, the infection could easily have been fatal. This is not a groundless fear as there have been many people murdered via medical neglect since COVID-19 began, being denied life-saving procedures such as organ transplants. It is not an uncommon belief that only the obedient deserve care and I worry that we may see a resurgence of these sentiments as the WHO inevitably declares pandemics, likely in the near future.

I have swallowed my share of Ivermectin – the kind that is formulated for horses – as it is harmless and despite the perfunctory disclaimer on the box, "not for human consumption", is effective for people. Many farmers will tell you that antibiotics are antibiotics, whether for animals or humans, and they have been successfully using animal medicine to treat themselves and their families for generations. Personally, I will be exercising more caution with these antibiotics than I do with the harmless Ivermectin because I know some people have reactions and/or develop antibiotic resistance due to overuse, so I intend to further educate myself on the matter. The following guide appears to be fairly comprehensive: Essential Guide To Fish Antibiotics for Humans (primalsurvivor.net). This is a gold mine for my preps and will be a wonderful supplement to this very comprehensive survival medicine book: The Survival Medicine Handbook: THE essential guide for when medical help is NOT on the way: Alton MD, Joseph, Alton ARNP, Amy: 9780988872554: Amazon.com: Books.

And as always, ask God for guidance. You can put your trust in Elon Musk who has ties to the WEF, fraternizes with Satanists, named his child "Darkside-rael", and is behind all the transhumanist technology. You can put your trust in Trump, though the swamp is deeper than ever and he continues to promote the genocide vaccines. You can cheer on Kanye West as the next Christian conservative champion although he just facilitated a worship session with Marilyn Manson and held an event that involved Bible-burning. But to me it seems all but impossible for billionaires to be servants of God and I wouldn't trust them for a second but rather would recommend that you trust in yourself, in the steps you've taken to prepare, and in God – that He will supplement your efforts.

I wouldn't bother mentioning preparation at all if I thought there were "white hats" making progress in this globalist war against humanity. I will not believe we are winning until vaccines are no longer mandatory for anything. I will not believe that we are winning until the truth is no longer demonized. I will not believe we are winning until a father can share that a vaccine killed his child without being censored online.

I understand these messages are not exactly hope-inspiring to some, but the truth is that there is no hope for the world. There is only hope for us individually in Christ. Secure your eternity in Him and it makes little difference to what extent the globalists are successful, not from a big-picture perspective. Once you're dead to the world, the world loses power over you, and to be alive in Christ is to be dead to the world. As humans, we are in a unique position such that we are tethered either to the world or to the spirit, and while we are alive, we choose our preference. The world is a sinking ship and Jesus is a hot air balloon. Tether yourself to the world and you will go down with it, but tether yourself to Jesus who defeated death, and you will ascend with Him even as the world meets its fate.

Newsletter 10 – Ancient Formula for Tyranny Now Unfolding

December 4, 2022

So much is happening in the world and yet I am at a loss for words as I run the risk of redundancy. Should I write about the war raging on? Should I write about looming energy shortages? Vaccine deaths continuing to increase? I likely can't tell you anything you don't already know at this point.

I suppose one new change is the censorship ramping up even farther. We knew this would occur as it's in the globalist battle plans and they have devoted a tremendous amount of time and resources into ensuring total narrative control. Content creators on social media are reporting suppression unlike any they've seen so far – mass reporting, comment deletion, algorithm sabotage resulting in little to no views, and account bans like never before. Why the sudden urgency? What are they gearing up for that they don't want people talking about?

The sad truth is that it could be a number of things. The very obviously stolen election is a subject deemed untouchable by our globalist overlords. Perhaps that's the reason for the notable censorship increase. The vaccine deaths are mounting and it seems to be increasingly difficult for them to cover it up. Maybe that's why. The destruction of efficient energy is demonstrating the stupidity of green policies and that is also an obvious fact that they cannot allow to be openly discussed. After all, that would be an affront to their earth-worshipping, anti-human religion.

Nobody can now deny that we are being ruled by Druidic pagans as they recently gathered at Mount Sinai (according to their calculations) to announce their own perverted moral code – the ten climate commandments. The blasphemy is becoming increasingly blatant. The COP27 symbol is intentionally reminiscent of the symbol for the ancient Egyptian sun god, Ra, and they even constructed their climate center (pagan temple) in the likeness of the symbol. This is not uninformed conjecture. In a Newsweek article penned by a COP27 member, homage was openly paid to Ra, who is a symbol for the all-seeing eye of Lucifer. You see, our Satanic leadership consider themselves gnostic followers of ancient mystery Babylon/Egypt. That is why we have pyramids capped with the all-seeing eye on our dollar bills.

The Euphrates River continues to dry up as red heifers are being assessed for suitability for the sacrifice at the apocalyptic 3rd temple, and some of the world's leading Rabbis are claiming to be in contact with the Jewish Messiah (the figure that Christians would call either The False Prophet or The Antichrist) who seems to have emerged from nowhere and is reportedly performing miracles. One-world government gains more footing even as the great river dries.

Perhaps to be taken with a few grains of salt, a long but frankly mind-blowing documentary called Europa may help shed some light on this emerging messiah figure. See it at https://www.bitchute.com/embed/YDyz9eZKkSQv/. I can't say I agree with every point made in a 11 to 12 hour documentary, but my mother always warned me not to throw the baby out with the bath water. Fair warning, it is not for the faint of heart. One may also gain some insight from perusing The Protocols of the Learned Elders of Zion, which can be found at NWOdocuments.com and reads like an antique playbook for installing a tyrannical new world order led by the Antichrist.

About 340 BC, Aristotle wrote about how to have a successful tyranny in one of his works on ethics:

The tyrant should lop off those who are too high and put to death mean of spirit. He must not allow common meals, clubs, education and the like. He must be upon his guard against anything that may inspire either courage or confidence amongst his subjects. He must prohibit assemblies and take every means to prevent people from knowing one another, for acquaintance begets mutual confidence. Further, he must compel all persons staying in the city to appear in public and live at his gates – then he will know what they are doing. If they are always kept under, they will learn to be humble... A tyrant should also endeavor to know what each of his subjects says or does and should employ spies... for the fear of informants prevents people from speaking their minds, and if they do, they are more easily found out. Another art of the tyrant is to sow quarrels among the citizens. Also, he should impoverish his subjects. He thus provides against the maintenance of the guard by the citizen, and the people, having to keep hard at work, are prevented from conspiring.

Let's break this down.

...put to death men of spirit. Who are men of spirit? Patriotic or religious people. People who would defy official narratives.

...must not allow common meals, clubs, education and the like. With the attack on food we have been seeing, our "common meals" may not be so common before long. And though we have a form of education, it is carefully tended by our government. One might say true education has been eradicated indeed.

...must be on his guard against anything that may inspire either courage or confidence amongst his subjects. One might say Hollywood leads the charge in the modern inspiration department, followed by propagandized media. Both entities are CIA-controlled. This has been demonstrated in congressional hearings decades ago. If you're waiting for a hero in any modern movie to be depicted as a patriotic Christian Conservative family man, don't hold your breath. They are certainly on guard against anything that may inspire

courage or confidence.

...further he must compel all persons staying in the city to appear in public and live at his gates. Have you heard about the 15-minute city project? It is being sold as a climate friendly way to structure a city such that all amenities are within proximity to all residents, but the true motivation is control. In a smart city of this kind, people would be monitored at all times and would be rendered immobile. A city such as this would make it very easy to ensure the people remain confined.

...a tyrant should also endeavor to know what each of his subjects says or does and should employ spies. That is precisely what fact-checkers and organizations like DHS's Disinformation Governance Board (which has NOT been disbanded as they claim) are for. Your devices are always listening.

...sow quarrels among the citizens. This has been successful enough in the 2-party system alone. Now add to that the race-baiting and false flag hate crimes to complement this division and we have quite a quarrelsome people indeed, which is much further exacerbated by social media.

...he should impoverish his subjects. This is naturally their goal. How many billions of dollars have gone to Ukraine, illegal immigration, and green policy money pits?

Perhaps most sobering, to me anyway, is that the thrust toward the installation of a medical dictatorship remains in full swing despite the now overwhelming evidence of medical fraud and the destruction wrought by WHO policies enforced by governments. British Columbia now seeks to penalize medical professionals who refuse vaccination, which is just another step toward mandating for the average citizen. I'm told a bill in California will be active January 1st which penalizes any doctor sharing the truth about vaccines – such as that they have damaged untold thousands, likely millions, of people, which is a demonstrable fact. And of course the international pandemic treaty has not gone away either. According to Dr. Francis Boyle, International law professor and expert on international treaties, the world could see a medical dictatorship as early as next May. Written into the fabric of the treaty is a pathway to bypass the necessity for senate approval. All it requires is the signature of a national leader in order to become immediately effective.

Sometimes things take so long I forget they're still a threat. I live in a headspace where everybody knows the vaccines are unsafe and ineffective and that COVID-19 was a power-grabbing charade and I forget that much of the rest of the world does not see it that way. Unthinkably, people are still in the throes of hypnotic suggestion, blindly absorbing the narratives impressed upon them by the despots who despise them. Yes, many are waking up, but the taproot of evil has already burrowed deeply and secured its place.

We know money is being laundered through Ukraine, yet they are still given billions of our dollars. We know Balenciaga is involved in the Satanic torture of children, but the great elite pedo ring continues to operate unfettered. We know Hunter Biden's laptop is authentic and proves that both he and our president are guilty of treason, yet Joe is still our president. We know that ballot machines across the nation (especially in key districts) "malfunctioned" during the midterm election, yet any resistance to the results will be overlooked just as they were following the 2020 Presidential election. We know vaccines are killing people, yet they're still being promoted and those who speak against it are still having their mouths stapled shut. We know that green policies are destroying our energy and our economy, yet we're still moving forward with them.

Don't worry though, there are good guys behind the scenes that have it all under control! Trust the plan! It only *looks* like we're being systematically destroyed. We'll vote them out during the next election! Trump or DeSantis will turn everything around! Elon Musk will save the world.

Yeah, okay. The only plan I trust is my own and God's. Unfortunately, I've read the books of prophecy and it gets real ugly. Stay armed and stay informed. Building community is the best thing we can do to survive. I hate to admit that as an introvert. Wishing you all the best as we continue to watch Aristotle's ancient formula for tyranny continue to unfold.

Newsletter 11 – Divorcing the Control Grid

December 24, 2022

I have successfully achieved another social media ban, this time immediately following a Tik Tok post that tied the Hollywood and political cults to organized Satanism and pedophilia, which is a well-known expression of Satanism. The question must be raised, why are our social engineers now endorsing child rape and torture? What does it mean when the rulership of a society works overtime to obfuscate crimes against children while promoting their sexualization?

We are ruled by Satanists at the very top and there are even some specific localities wherein these degenerate wastes of oxygen have secured absolute control. I refer the reader to the Hampstead case, now dismissed as an honest misunderstanding as these kinds of situations often miraculously manage to be.

The police interviews may still be viewable online. To summarize, two young children, brother and sister, came forward and reported in minute detail what they had been experiencing at the Christ Church school in Hampstead. Their stories did not conflict with one another. They described how they would be taken into the chapel by their teachers and their father, how they would "do sex" with "plastic willies" and the adults would help them kill babies that they would then eat.

The interviews lasted hours and the children answered every question asked, never wavering, though the technique of the interviewer was questionable. Following the police report and subsequent interviews, there was no follow-up with any of the alleged offenders who the children identified by name. Rather, the children were released back to their mother and later called back in for a second interview, during which they retracted their incredibly detailed, corresponding accounts. Clearly, they had been coached to recant.

If they had made the whole thing up (for no reason), I wonder how it is that upon medical examination, both children were found to have sustained significant sexual damage. This fact was somehow not mentioned when the mainstream media, ever dutiful to their dark overlords, put the children's demonic father on full display in a televised interview to lament how hurtful it was for him to undergo such baseless accusations from his own children. And if one were to now seek information online pertaining to the Hampstead case, they'd be bombarded with fact-checks that, as is customary, always seem to play damage control for atrocities such as these.

Consider for a moment what this implies. There is an entire city so controlled by Satanists that the schools, police force, and judges are all involved, allowing them to operate with impunity. The word "occult" means "hidden". It follows that occult practices are far more ubiquitous than most would dare believe. An authority on this subject once stated that there is a coven in nearly every town across the country, and they don't just sit in their basements holding seances, they infiltrate communities, particularly public office and the church. It is not difficult to masquerade as a Christian. And of course nobody is wise to it because the occult keeps things occult.

If you're new to this subject matter, I can assure you, it is very real and only the tip of the iceberg. In doing some cursory research, I found a record of events similar to those of the Hampstead case, but close to where I currently reside. A coven sacrificed someone to Satan and although several people were clearly indicated, only one person was penalized for it. But do you suppose anybody knows about it? Of course not. These things are swept under the rug and any mention of them is derisively termed, "satanic panic", a weaponized phrase meant to discredit facts in the same fashion that the

CIA's phrase, "conspiracy theory" is intended to. Their allegiance to stifling the truth is diabolical.

So when I am called a defeatist for expressing my opinion that this country has met its end, I assume my accuser just lacks familiarity with the extent of the malignancy that permeates our nation. When one is inclined toward seeking political solutions to the Hellish circus we now find ourselves in, it is all but certain that the two-party charade has been programmed into their minds and they still have faith in the system, that if only the right candidate was elected (as if elections are real), we could finally get out of this mess.

To highlight the hopelessness of this position, I call attention to the recent visit from gay porn actor, Volodymyr Zelensky to Washington DC, whereupon he received a standing ovation from everyone present, Democrats and Republicans alike. There was no talk of peace. Just more encouragement to continue the war so that American politicians can continue to send Ukraine taxpayer dollars (Zelensky promised the funds were being used responsibly, providing no data to validate his claims) so that they can be laundered back into their pockets, though with a few more blood stains on them.

The Uniparty is alive and well. Partisan opposition is a farce to keep the people hopeful and complacent while they are being destroyed in plain view. The attack is multifaceted and complex. There is a social degradation component as evidenced by the promotion of pedophilia under the guise of tolerance, there is the encroaching digital currency that will enable social credit, there is the system of medical tyranny still being vigorously worked on by the WHO and member states of the International Health Regulations, there is the provocation of war, the destruction of food via the vilification of agriculture, and so much more.

One of the worst things is that it is beginning to feel normal to me. I have no strong desire to return to social media and continue to plead my case. It is beginning to feel increasingly more as though those who don't see what's coming simply don't want to and therefore never will. My impulse to persuade others of the dangers we are facing is waning, and I am not alone in this. A content creator on Tik Tok recently expressed similar sentiments. Her drive to warn the willfully ignorant is taking a back seat to her drive to establish a community of like-minded people and live as independently of the system as possible. People are having an instinct pulling them toward the cover of foliage, plunging their RV deep into the woods somewhere and hiding, setting up an off-grid homestead. You are likely no exception.

Perhaps the season of warning is coming to an end and the season of preparation is at hand, though rather than being exclusively a spiritual movement, these sentiments are no doubt driven in part by the incessant silencing of our voices. Nonetheless, many of us are now intuiting that the time to separate from society is drawing near. That said, I am no seer, and had I acted on my intuition when the pandemic fraud was first initiated, I'd have been living in a hut in the woods needlessly for the past 3 years. The timing is the wild card. Nobody knows exactly when this transition to a new way of life will become finally necessary. My thought is that with whatever remaining time we have, it may be wise to use much of it to make efforts toward building community.

The question is how to do it. We're more dependent on the system than most of us think. We rely almost exclusively on technology to communicate, and even if we communicate via snail mail, that is dependence on the system as well – though more reliable as any technological device you use is assuredly watching your every move. It is necessary that any established locations remain known only to those directly involved. Trust is a must. I may trust Person A with whom I am making plans, but not the people with whom Person A is communicating.

For this reason, it seems to me that relatively small, tightly knit groups may be the best option to begin with.

We are dealing with provocateurs as we have seen in the January 6th operation. These people, like the occult, infiltrate the forces of good, pretending to be something they are not. And they are legion as evidenced by the suspicious hiring of 87,000 IRS agents trained to use deadly force and the thousands of people hired to combat "misinformation". The enemy is building an army and I have no doubt they will make every effort to infiltrate their opposition. So again, the question is one of how to build a community while excluding possible moles who would gleefully disclose your location to the nearest antihuman authority at the first opportunity.

This can be challenging as many people who may provide a good deal of value in a community may also fit the profile of a Fed – usually fit, likely type-A personality, possible military history. A greater threat of infiltration exists when attempting to build a community from the basis of social media where enemy infiltrators exist in greater numbers. We can be certain from their own globalist literature that monumental efforts are being made to identify and root out freedom lovers, especially online, so these are not paranoid delusions of persecution when said persecution is clearly defined in their game plans.

I would like to believe that complete self-subsistence is achievable, but in a police state system, operating as a part of a community would significantly increase chances of survival. That said, perhaps preparing on an individual level is a necessary first step to developing such a community. Either someone with adequate acreage must fully own their property to provide a starting point while everyone else's property is getting confiscated by the banks, or there must be sufficient organization such that it is feasible to retreat as a group into the deep recesses of the millions of acres of unexplored forest that the government claims to own via state and national parks. There are probably some alternative options, but those are the two most prominent in my mind

All planning must take into consideration the likelihood of having no access to medical services, food, housing, or clean water, and even the possibility of having been declared an eco-fascist or some such terrorist threat and, worst case scenario, being sought by the authorities. They aren't building camps just to leave them empty. They aren't implying that people with Christian ideals are terrorist threats only to later change their minds and decide that we're really not so bad after all. This is a concerted, slow rolling plan being constructed brick by brick until one day we notice the wall has become too high to scale and we should have trusted our first instinct to flee but were kept just comfortable enough not to.

Still, if it ever starts to feel hopeless, remember that in the end, we win.

And I say also unto thee, that thou art Peter, and upon this rock I will build my church; and the gates of hell shall not prevail against it. -Matthew 16:18

Newsletter 12 – Tragedy Unfolding

December 26, 2022

William Shatner has been part of the Hollywood elite for decades. During an interview following his return from his trip to space (an obsession of the elites) he made mention of a "coming catastrophic event". Wonder what he meant.

Could it have anything to do with the Deagel Report? If you're not familiar with it, the Deagel Report projects future data, such as that of the global population. It has been known to be so accurate that the United States government did or does reference it for their own purposes. Oddly, the report suggested without explanation that many populations, most acutely those of Western nations, would see a devastating reduction in the year 2025, the United States seeing the most dramatic population shift, from 324 million to 54 million, followed by the United Kingdom and other Western nations. Some have noted that the percentage of the population reductions closely mirror the percentage of those who received the mRNA vaccinations. Whether it be that, a nuclear holocaust, large scale starvation, or any number of unfortunately viable explanations, it seems as though something may be on the horizon within that time frame, especially considering that the Globalists often indicate the year 2025 in their documentation. Shatner certainly expects an impending cataclysm of sorts.

Perhaps it will be a convergence of the aforementioned possibilities. They do all relate to one another in some way. The vaccination theory makes sense as according to some of the mRNA studies, the test animals perished in a time frame proportional to 3-5 human years. Based on that, if on average, wide scale vaccination began early 2021, one could expect more alarming damages to begin emerging in 2024, possibly causing the dramatic population reduction projected in the

Deagel Report by 2025. I make no guarantee that that is the case, but the timelines add up.

I find it very telling that even as data that exposes the true nature of these "vaccines" continues to emerge and even slowly becomes increasingly integrated into the mainstream, still the silencing and censorship persists. The fastest way to get a video deleted or even a permanent ban remains to mention that the vaccines could maybe possibly not be entirely safe, though at this point that is a verifiable fact. That Big Tech remains complicit in murder via vaccine by silencing those who care to warn others is alarming. It's the equivalent of holding someone's mouth shut so they can't warn a hiker in front of them to watch their step because there's a hidden pitfall that many are known to succumb to. And on a related note, Satanic globalist Elon Musk has done nothing that caused any actual harm to the globalist agenda at all. Color me surprised.

But Edward Dowd has. Dowd, a Wall Street careerist who worked for Black Rock, found considerable success in his ability to analyze statistics and identify trends early. He became interested in some of the data on sudden, unexplained deaths that began to emerge in 2021 and drew together a team to study the phenomenon and ultimately publish his findings in a book entitled, "Cause Unknown: The Epidemic of Sudden Deaths in 2021 and 2022".

I've found that one of the best ways to experience censorship on social media is to merely mention this book. In it, Dowd includes a wealth of unassailable evidences for the fact that this scourge of sudden deaths is anything but ordinary and that only the mandatory vaccination campaign can be responsible. Dowd puts the phenomenon into context: *From February 2021 to March 2022, millennials experienced the equivalent of a Vietnam war, with more than 60,000 excess deaths. The Vietnam war took 12 years to kill the same number of healthy young people we've see die in 12 months.*

The CEO of OneAmerica insurance company disclosed that deaths among working age people increased 40% and a majority of these were not attributed to COVID. Dowd notes that even just a 10% increase in excess deaths would be a 1 in 200-year event.

Many denial artists maintain that these deaths are normal, especially among athletes. The healthiest people in the world always regularly drop dead. But Gary Dempsey stated that he was a professional footballer for nearly 20 years and since 1996 he's played nearly 500 games. He notes that "Never ever was there one cardiac arrest. Either in the crowd or a player. It's actually quite scary."

Dowd shares some of the best evidence to rebut the normalcy bias we hear from so many brainwashed automatons these days, citing a study that determined that there had been 1,101 cases of sudden cardiac deaths in athletes over the course of 38 years, which is an average of about 29 per year. He notes that since June 2021 there hasn't been even one month with fewer than 29 such deaths and that there were 90 reported in December 2021 alone.

Dowd also defeats the desperate claim that these deaths must be from "long COVID", a term recently invented to mask the myriad of vaccine damages. *Cause Unknown* includes a number of graphs developed from data gleaned by reputable research establishments that provides a clear correlation between the vaccination program and the unprecedented increase in sudden deaths. The denial artists cry, "Correlation doesn't equal causation!" but of course it often does. One could make the same denialist claim that just because Person X was just hit by a dump truck, that doesn't mean that's what killed him. Correlation doesn't equal causation after all. Perhaps Person X had a heart attack just before getting hit. Now multiply that singular coincidence by several thousand and you've entered the delusional mind of those fools so desperate to believe that any data point that makes them uncomfortable is simply an outlier.

Take into account the numbers above presented by Dowd as you peruse the victims of the Malthusian globalist agenda below. Take also into account that these are largely young, healthy individuals, the group that is historically least likely to experience excess mortality but are now inexplicably (it's very explainable actually) in the most danger of premature death. Somehow, people who are working age (mandated to receive vaccination in order to retain employment) are now suddenly dying without explanation, and this is demonstrated over and over again by those who are highly motivated to produce painstakingly accurate data regarding excess mortality – life insurance companies.

See below. It is what it looks like.

[A litany of charts demonstrating vaccine-caused deaths]

As you can see, these data sets are from the Johns Hopkins University Coronavirus Resource Center, an organization that, if anything, would be motivated to at least minimize the appearance of harmful effects of mass vaccination, however, the data at this point are plainly insurmountable. I can only imagine the glee on the faces of our depopulationist overlords as they review their progress so clearly outlined in charts such as these. Still, the public will declare the vaccines safe and effective while they demonize those who dare to so much as mention the obvious.

In his book, Dowd explains his rationale for presenting the cases that he does (some of which are depicted below) and that these represent only the tip of the iceberg. And as previously mentioned, this amount of excess death is not anywhere near the usual rate despite the brainless cries to the contrary.

[A litany of "died suddenly" articles]

To view each news report in more detail, simply use your camera phone to scan the QR codes which conveniently take you directly to the article. True, many of these do not directly cite the vaccine as the cause of death. Of course they wouldn't. But you'll notice many of these individuals fall under the category of people who would be mandated to receive vaccination in order to maintain their careers – those in whose deaths insurance companies have noted an extreme uptick that defies statistical probability. Also, don't forget the data cited above, nor the graphs that paint the picture as vividly as possible.

These stories constitute only a minute subset of data that represent the totality of deaths wrought since 2021 which even now has overshadowed the worst wars in history, but worse yet, continue to mount. Normally I would shake my head and move on, knowing that many people already comprehend our current situation and those who don't have simply chosen not to and never will. But many of you are made of a different material. The kind of person that subscribes to a site like this and takes the time to read emails like these is more inclined to utilize resources for truth to further God's cause, to proliferate the human race, the antithesis of the globalist antihuman agenda. Therefore, it's worth my time to share this information with you whether or not you share it directly with anyone else, if for no other reason than to strengthen your arguments against these euthanasia injections and reassure you – as if you need to be reassured – that you are correct beyond a shadow of a doubt.

Now for the real nightmare. If it is true that the real vaccine fallout will not even begin to occur until 2024, then even the thousands of deaths we have seen thus far are only a molehill beside the mountain of death still to occur. Only two years remain to validate or invalidate the projections of the Deagel report. As we approach another pandemic treaty vote to cede authority from nations to the WHO as early as May, the stage may be getting set for Gates's "Pandemic 2", which could simply be the side-effects of the COVID injections finally manifesting, but could also conceivably be a bioweapon release. They aren't investing in gain-of-function research for nothing.

As always, time will tell.

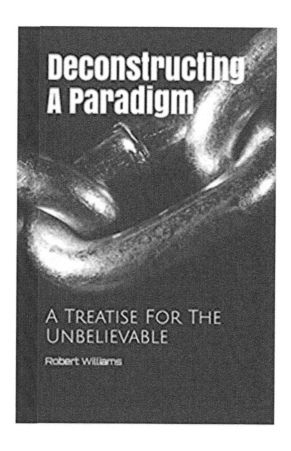

Deconstructing A Paradigm takes an apologetic approach to phenomena that the general public often regards with skepticism. It offers a combination of hard-to-refute evidences and well-reasoned rationale for the existence of such things as an afterlife realm, spiritual beings, conspiracies, extraterrestrial life, and many other things that the general mind-controlled population has no comprehension of. Turn through the pages to learn more about the true nature of the realm you inhabit. Find it on Amazon.com.

Should we continue to accept the currently understood etiology of addiction? How much faith should we place in the prevailing treatment models for chemical dependency? How is one truly able to recover from addiction? *Addiction and Recovery* will assist the reader in considering such questions. Find it on Amazon.com.

Kopf

Made in the USA
Middletown, DE
07 February 2023

24243237R00156